Speaking of Divorce

How to Talk with Your Kids and Help Them Cope

Roberta Beyer and Kent Winchester

Edited by Marjorie Lisovskis

free spirit
PUBLiSHiNG®

Works
for kids®

Library of Congress Cataloging-in-Publication Data

Beyer, Roberta, 1951–
    Speaking of divorce : how to talk with your kids and help them cope / Roberta Beyer and Kent Winchester.
      p. cm.
    Also issued as a component of a kit entitled Juggling act.
    Includes bibliographical references and index.
    ISBN 1-57542-093-7 (pbk.)
      1. Divorced parents. 2. Children of divorced parents. 3. Divorce—Psychological aspects. 4. Parent and child. I. Winchester, Kent. II. Title.

HQ759.915 .B48 2001
306.89—dc21

2001023030

At the time of this book's publication, all facts and figures cited are the most current available; all telephone numbers, addresses, and Web site URLs are accurate and active; all publications, organizations, Web sites, and other resources exist as described in this book; and all have been verified. The authors and Free Spirit Publishing make no warranty or guarantee concerning the information and materials given out by organizations or content found at Web sites, and we are not responsible for any changes that occur after this book's publication. If you find an error or believe that a resource listed here is not as described, please contact Free Spirit Publishing. Parents, teachers, and other adults: We strongly urge you to monitor children's use of the Internet.

Illustrations by Marieka Heinlen
Index compiled by Randl Ockey

10 9 8 7 6 5 4 3 2
Printed in Canada

Free Spirit Publishing Inc.
217 Fifth Avenue North, Suite 200
Minneapolis, MN 55401-1299
(612) 338-2068
help4kids@freespirit.com
www.freespirit.com

Speaking of Divorce

How to Talk with Your Kids and Help Them Cope

Dedication

For our parents

Acknowledgments

We have many people to acknowledge in writing this book. We wish to thank the staff of the Court Clinic at the Second Judicial District Court in Albuquerque, New Mexico, for their suggestions and insight, especially Dr. Louise Kodituwaaku, Clinical Director. These professionals work tirelessly on behalf of families.

We are indebted to Jan Zimmerman who encouraged us all along the way and who believed in the projects related to children of divorce.

We are grateful to Judge Anne Kass of the Second Judicial District Court in Albuquerque, New Mexico. Many of the ideas in this book came from her and she graciously encouraged us to use them. Anne has helped innumerable families through the divorce process and bettered countless children's lives.

We also want to thank Shelly for all her assistance and patience with the innumerable drafts and changes to this book. Thanks also to our helpers who know who they are.

Contents

Foreword

As a judge in a divorce court for more than fifteen years and as a divorce attorney for seven years prior to that, I have learned many valuable lessons. Perhaps the most important is from *Life's Little Instruction Book,* which advises: "Never cut what can be untied."* This is a wise goal for divorcing parents. Divorce does not end a relationship—it only changes it. For two people who have a child together, "till death do us part" is a description of unavoidable reality.

Many divorcing parents desperately want their spouse to disappear from their lives, but the reality is that a former spouse doesn't become a "former" parent. Though the couple's connection to each other may be over, the one to their children remains. What this means for the divorcing couple is that they are forever linked through their children. As this fact begins to sink in, angry frustration often becomes the permanent theme in parents' interactions. Divorce itself does not have to do lasting damage to children, but bitter hostility between divorced parents will. Though they may not realize it and certainly do not intend it, parents who continue in high conflict (whether by heated, intense interactions or by icy, cold silence) do harm to their children and, of course, to themselves.

During my years as a practicing attorney I realized that my clients often ended up "worse off" after court divorce proceedings. Frequently they were angrier and always poorer, even if they had technically "won" in court. I asked myself the Great American

---

* *Life's Little Instruction Book: 511 Reminders for a Happy and Rewarding Life* by H. Jackson Brown Jr., Nashville, TN: Rutledge Hill Press, 1991, instruction 245.

Question: Whose fault is it? As an attorney, I decided judges were to blame because they were scared to make tough decisions and didn't understand families. When I became a family court judge in 1984, I adopted a tough, no-nonsense attitude and ordered parents to behave. After a few years of that, I realized that it, too, was not working very well. So again, I asked myself whose fault it was. This time I decided attorneys who were afraid to deliver bad news to their clients were to blame.

Then I attended a week-long conference on mediation training. I finally began to recognize that problem solving, not winning, should be the goal. I learned that I needed to stop polarized thinking—thinking only in terms of right and wrong, winning and losing. I stopped indulging in the "fault fantasy" and quit assigning blame. I realized that we blame people only to shift the focus from ourselves.

Since then I have seen thousands of divorcing couples in my courtroom, I know that they are scared and in pain. I know that it is difficult for them to stay in a positive frame of mind. Many wonder, "Why me?" Often they answer that question by blaming the other person. I try to help them see what my lengthy experience in family law has taught me: You can either fix the blame or fix the problem. You can't do both. And fixing the blame never works. It is better by far to solve the problems caused by divorce than it is to assign blame. I want the couples in my courtroom, and you, to know that this period of life offers the opportunity to grow and to ask a much better question: What could be good about the divorce?

The book you are about to read is designed to help divorcing parents untie their marriage—to make the transition from one home to two, where kindness toward and respect for the other are the standard. If you are able to incorporate all or some of the suggestions from the pages that follow into your divorce process, your children will not merely survive your breakup—they will flourish from the life skills you will have modeled for them.

I wish you all the best.

Judge Anne Kass
Albuquerque, New Mexico

Introduction

If you are reading these words, it must be a difficult time in your life and the life of your family. Whether you are already divorced, in the process of divorcing, or considering a divorce, this book will help you think about how the divorce will affect your children.

Divorce ends a marriage, yet it does not and cannot end a family. Your children are always going to be your children, and your divorce is going to have long-lasting effects on them. We wrote *Speaking of Divorce* to provide you with information about those effects and to recommend ways you can talk with your children, gently but truthfully, about the divorce.

Many of the suggestions we make will be difficult for you and your ex-spouse to accept. This is not a time when it's easy to cooperate with your children's other parent. You may not have wanted a divorce and may be feeling shocked and betrayed. You may have bitter feelings toward your ex-spouse, and long for a time when you don't need to communicate with each other at all. You may be lonely, confused, and hurt. Anger may be your constant companion. Guilt may spring out unexpectedly every day. Often, you'll find yourself with little energy left for parenting. All divorces bring with them varying degrees of unpleasant, uncomfortable, even painful emotions for you and for your children. Nonetheless, this is a time when parents can have a tremendous positive impact on the lives of their children. Throughout this book we will talk about your children's future and what you can do now to affect that future in positive ways.

What your children need from you

A fundamental truth is that your children need two loving parents. They need two parents who are able to cooperate in raising them, no matter how you and your ex-spouse may feel about each other. Though your marriage is dissolved, your commitment to your children remains—in fact, your kids need you now more than ever. Part of doing what's best for children is to contain the hostility that will arise from time to time toward your former spouse. Handling the post-divorce years with dignity and respect for one another will go a long way toward helping your children to better futures.

Children are resilient. Current research on the long-term effects of divorce strongly suggests that children are most likely to weather the divorce well when the level of conflict and hostility between their parents is low. If the level is high, children won't do as well.

Besides the animosity that divorcing couples feel, other barriers can arise. Divorce changes parenting responsibilities. Prior to the separation, one parent may have handled most of the day-to-day parenting tasks, and so the other parent may not know as much about how to parent and coparent. Parents may also have had differences during the marriage about issues surrounding children's schoolwork, household chores, bedtimes, allowances, social activities, and behavior. One parent may have been stricter, the other more permissive. These concerns all become part of the challenge parents face as they work to cooperate in caring for their kids during and after the divorce.

You are your child's most important role model. That extends to how you communicate with the other parent as well as how you resolve conflicts with that parent. You will probably be together at your children's graduations, weddings, and other major life events. Many adult children tell sad stories about how they could not invite both parents to their weddings for fear of the scenes that might happen. One of the most loving things you can do for your children is to work on a positive relationship with the other parent.

We understand that this ideal is not always possible. Situations that mandate a different kind of parenting do exist. Some parents desert their children. Some are abusive. Many don't pay child support. Others are simply ignorant of what needs to be done for their children. Yet it's in nearly all children's best interests for parents to cooperate in raising them.

We hope that your children's other parent is as interested in easing the negative effects of divorce as you are. We hope both of you will read this book. A thoughtful approach to coparenting insures a better future for your children, both now and when they enter their own adult relationships. Nonetheless, you may be parenting alone, and wondering whether this book can help you. It can. If cooperation and positive communication between the two of you aren't possible, the ideas presented in *Speaking of Divorce* will help you support and reassure your children while doing all you can to shield them from the adult problems between you and your ex. In addition, we suggest ways to talk about an absent parent that may help if you are compelled to parent alone.

The reality is, unless your children are seriously mistreated while in the care of their other parent, there's little you can do to affect your ex-spouse's parenting skills or practices. Your ex will parent in his or her own style, sometimes doing and saying things you'll disagree with. Moreover, the legal system cannot resolve most parenting disputes. Neither the courts nor you can change your ex-spouse.

What you *can* do is decide how you will handle the situation as it exists. For the sake of your kids, you can take the high road. Difficult as this may be, it will lead to a better life for your children—and for you. Your efforts to conduct yourself with grace now can yield later rewards. When the pain and sorrow of this moment are no more than a memory, your children will honor and thank you.

How to use this book

We wrote *Speaking of Divorce* to help you—alone or with your ex-spouse—guide your children through your breakup and its aftermath. Much of what we recommend in these pages is geared to parents of kids ages seven to twelve. A good deal of the information can apply to younger and older children, too. We designed the book to be helpful and to the point, not overwhelming. It's compact enough that you can read it from cover to cover if you wish, or keep it on hand and read it a bit at a time. We've arranged the book by topics headed with simple affirmations. For each topic, the book frames the issue, gives important background information along with points for you to consider, and suggests language you can use to begin explaining particular subjects to children and answering their questions. At the end of the book you'll find a glossary of divorce terms and descriptions of books, Web sites, and organizations that can point you to more information and support. Use the index to help you find specific topics of concern.

Though helpful on its own, this book is part of a divorce survival kit for families called *Juggling Act: Handling Divorce Without Dropping the Ball*. The kit includes *What in the World Do You Do When Your Parents Divorce?*

(a book for elementary-aged children), The Mom & Dad Pad (a tool for parent-to-parent communication), and a "Keep Track" calendar and stickers for kids. These materials are described at the back of this book.

Speaking of Divorce is shaped around the particular needs of children whose families are divorcing or divorced. What do these children need?

1. They need permission to love *both* parents.

2. They need you to tell them what is happening—patiently, honestly, and in a way that's appropriate for their age and level of development.

3. They need to know that divorce is a grown-up problem and that it is *not* their fault.

4. They need to be able to ask questions and talk about their worries, fears, and other feelings. They need to know that their parents will listen to them and hear what they say. They need to know where to go when they want to talk with someone other than a parent.

5. They need stability and predictability.

6. They need hugs, support, and love.

This is a time of enormous change for you and your children. Big changes are always stressful. They can also be exhilarating. Your children will learn much from what you say to them now and what your actions show them.

Roberta Beyer and Kent Winchester

"We're getting divorced"

Tell the truth in an age-appropriate way.

All human beings need to know that they *belong*, that there is a place for them on this earth. For children, that place is in a home—or homes—with their parents. Children whose parents are divorcing need the security of knowing that they will remain part of a loving family, but divorce can seriously undermine that security.

The emotional hurricane that blows through children's lives during and after a divorce can be devastating, but it does not have to be. You will have tremendous influence on how your children weather the breakup. By sharing information honestly and straightforwardly, you'll reassure them that they're safe. By telling them—over and over—that they are important, that you love them, and that you won't stop loving them, you will anchor them through the storm of their parents' divorce.

Your children will remember forever how, when, and what you told them about the end of your marriage. It will be one of the most important conversations in their lives. The good news is that this occasion will give you a powerful opportunity to begin helping your children through the divorce in a *positive* way. Children need to know what will happen to them, that they're not the cause of the divorce, and that their parents will still love them. When you tell your kids about the divorce, you have your first chance to help them understand these things.

Telling your children about your breakup is hard, but it's critical that you do so in a planned, thoughtful manner. Many well-meaning parents delay this conversation too long. Some believe that they're sparing their children pain by not telling them as soon as the decision is made. Often, guilt or fear keeps a parent from initiating this conversation. Though this is understandable, waiting until the last minute is more damaging than telling children the truth promptly.

Many children whose parents are divorced complain that no one told them at the time what was happening or why. Often they learned about the breakup on the day that Mom or Dad moved out. Imagine how frightening this would be to a child. Learning, with little or no warning, that the family is going to change in such a fundamental way can shatter children's sense of security, increase their anxiety, and contribute to a lack of trust in their parents and in the world.

You may be in a situation where it's not possible to tell your children in advance. Your partner may have moved out one day with no warning. If this is the case, talk with your kids about what has happened honestly and as reassuringly as you can, without saying negative things about the absent parent. For example, you might say: "Dad has moved out. It happened really fast, and we both feel very bad. I'm sorry you didn't know what was going on—it's a grown-up problem between the two of us, but I wish we'd told you sooner." Let your children know that they can talk to each of you when they want to, and do all you can to enlist your spouse in talking together with you and the children about the divorce. If your child has been surprised because her other parent moved out suddenly, you'll need to make an extra effort over the next weeks and months to reassure her that you love her and will provide a safe and secure home for her.*

---

* In *Speaking of Divorce,* we alternate in referring to individual kids as "she" or "he." Unless a specific note is made, the information presented applies to both boys *and* girls.

If you and your spouse are separating rather than divorcing, it's equally important to tell your children what will be happening. You might begin by saying, "We've agreed it's better for the two of us not to live together for a while. We might decide to get a divorce, or we might decide to get back together. We'll tell you when we have made the decision. In the meantime, we'll be living apart and you'll spend time with both of us."

Guidelines for telling your kids about the divorce

Here are some general guidelines for explaining your divorce to your kids; we elaborate on many of the suggestions and points later in the book. How much you tell your children and how you say it will depend on their ages and levels of maturity. If you're separating rather than divorcing, follow the same general guidelines.

1. Both of you should be present. Even if your breakup is unpleasant and difficult, put that aside and talk *together* with your children. It's important for you to appear calm and confident during this conversation. Children need to know that their parents can be trusted and relied on, even in a crisis.

Arrange a time for this talk when your home is quiet: turn off the TV and radio and make sure the phone won't ring. Sit facing the children and, especially with younger kids, touch them or hold their hand while you talk with them.

If you have to tell the children about the divorce by yourself

If, for whatever reason, your spouse won't be present when you tell the children about your divorce, keep the following in mind.

- Don't blame the other parent.

- Assure children that they'll continue to see both of you (if this is true).

- Tell them you know they love their other parent and that this is okay.

- Tell them it's fine to ask both you and the other parent questions.

- Tell them the decision was mutual: "Your dad/mom and I both agree we can't live together."

2. Talk to all of your children at the same time. If you have more than one child, have this conversation with all of the kids at once. Over time, you'll want and need to have separate talks with each child, but it's important that they be together when they hear the news for the first time. If you first explain the divorce to children individually, problems may arise that will complicate and confuse the situation. For example, parents may tell an older child first and ask him not to talk to his younger siblings before they do. The unintended result can be that the older child gets the message the divorce is secretive and that his family can't be straightforward in discussing it. If the information filters down to the younger children anyway, they often feel left out and even more worried about what's happening.

3. Be honest and give appropriate information. Explain that you're divorcing and will be living in two different places. Let your kids know that you tried hard to work things out but weren't able to stay together. Say you're sorry the marriage didn't work out, but that you're doing what's right for both of you. If you worked with someone before deciding to divorce (such as a counselor or member of the clergy), tell them that. Let them know this was not an easy decision for either of you.

Your purpose is to tell your children what's happening and how it will affect them, and to reassure them that you'll take care of them and meet their needs. It's not appropriate for children to hear the adult issues between you and your spouse. For example, if only one of you wants the divorce and the other doesn't, this isn't information you'll want to share with the kids. One partner's decision to end a marriage will result in a breakup even if the other partner doesn't want it. The truth that children need to hear in this situation is that the marriage didn't work and that their parents are sorry and sad that it's ending.

4. Tell children the divorce is *not* their fault. It's likely that your children will believe they did something that caused the divorce. It may sound strange, but it's almost universally true that children blame themselves for their parents' divorce. Tell them, now and repeatedly, that the breakup is not their fault. They will need to hear this important message again and again for a long time. (See pages 19–24 for more about this issue.)

5. Reassure them of your love. Children often fear that because their mom and dad stopped loving each other, they may stop loving *them,* too. Tell your kids that even though adults sometimes stop loving each other or quit living together, they never stop loving their children. Tell them how happy you both were when they came into your lives. Reassure them that parents *never* stop loving their children, even when they don't stay married. If the other parent is absent or won't have contact with the children for now, tell the children that this parent loves them, too. You might say: "Mommy isn't here now, but even though she's gone, I know she loves you."

6. Talk about the living plan. Let the kids know that you'll work out all the details of where they'll live and what their schedule with both of you will be. If you've already set a schedule, tell them generally what it will be. Explain that you'll listen to their feelings about the new living arrangements. Don't ask them who they want to live with or how much time they want to spend with each of you. Make it clear that you are responsible for these kinds of decisions.

Give children as much information as you can about the plans for living arrangements, moves, and schedules. They'll have concrete worries about matters like bedrooms, pets, toys, friends, and activities. Reassure them that you'll do your best to disrupt their lives as little as possible.

Ideally, if you have more than one child, you'll also want to tell your kids that you won't separate them from each other. Many children report that having a sibling was one of the most important things that helped them through the divorce. If you're thinking about separating your kids, we suggest talking to a qualified counselor before you do.

7. Ask your children what they want to know. Encouraging questions during this conversation is also important. Many children, especially younger ones, don't understand divorce. They will have many misconceptions and worries. Some parents assume they know what their kids are thinking and feeling, only to find that children had entirely different concerns. For example, one couple carefully explained to their daughter how they would get her to and from school. The girl listened with a sorrowful frown, saying nothing and appearing not to hear. The child's father then said, "I can see you're upset. Are you worried about having two different school-bus routes?" The daughter responded by asking where the family dog would live. "I always walk Buttons after school," she said. "What will happen if I'm not here for him?" Invite your children to ask questions and tell you what worries them. Let them know they can ask about whatever's bothering them whenever they want to.

8. Don't play the "blame game." Getting through this conversation with your children is going to be difficult for both of you, especially if your kids are asking why you're getting divorced. You'll want to answer their questions honestly, but you won't want to share adult issues with them or put them in the middle of your disputes. It's crucial that you and your ex not appear to blame each other for the divorce. Keep in mind how important it is for your children to feel that they can love and be loved by both parents. Blaming the other parent can feel to your children as if you're blaming *them.*

Revealing details about disagreements, making rude or sarcastic remarks, sighing, or sitting in angry silence are all highly visible signs to your children. Witnessing their parents' hostility or sense of betrayal can cause long-term problems for them. If the reasons for the divorce do include adult issues like arguments or affairs, tell children that there are grown-up matters you're not going to share with them. Don't lie—simply recognize that there's some information that shouldn't be shared with children, who have loyalties to both parents and aren't emotionally or intellectually equipped to handle many of the adult concerns that arise in divorces.

It's important that you try your best to be matter-of-fact in this dialogue. Doing this, and figuring out how to answer questions truthfully without overloading children with information they don't want or need, is quite a challenge. When you plan this conversation, you might start by asking yourself: "What does my child need to know here? How can I explain it in a way that's appropriate for him to hear?" To the best of your ability, try to predict the most likely questions. For example, a child may ask his mother, "Why is Daddy moving out? Are you mad at him?" The mother may be very angry with Daddy, who had an affair and hurt her deeply. What she can honestly tell the child is this: "Daddy and Mommy have some grown-up problems. We're not going to tell you about things that are private to us. We both feel very bad about this, and we've agreed we can't live together anymore."

If you've made some mistakes in talking to your kids

It's possible that you're already separated or divorced and don't feel you've explained things to your children as sensitively as you could have. Maybe you worry that you sent mixed messages, or regret remarks you made about their other parent. If you're in this situation, take steps now to start talking with your kids more supportively. If possible, sit down together with the children and the other parent. You might start the conversation by saying, "It must have been pretty hard for you when Mom and I broke up. I don't think we explained the divorce to you as clearly as we should have, and we may have said some things that upset or confused you. We're sorry about that, and we'd like to talk with you about it."

9. Listen and observe. When they hear about the divorce, children will have many emotions. They may feel worried, sad, angry, confused, torn, surprised, or even relieved. Some kids may not appear, on the surface, to feel much of anything. They simply may have shut down in order to protect themselves. This doesn't mean that they aren't having strong feelings or aren't affected by the news. In fact, they may be so overwhelmed that they cannot deal with the situation at that moment. Each child absorbs information differently. Pay close attention and respond to what you hear and see—to children's words, tone of voice, facial expressions, and body language. Be guided by these signals. If your children express emotions during this talk, listen and acknowledge their feelings. If they seem "tuned out," give them time and promise to talk to them again soon. Signal by *your* words, tone of voice, facial expressions, and body language that you are there for them and willing to talk whenever they need to.

10. Talk with your kids again and again. Once you've told your children about the divorce, expect to have many more conversations, both planned and impromptu, over the coming weeks, months, and even years. If your child seems extremely distraught or visibly unaffected, talk again soon. Talking won't fix everything—there are as many different ways to process emotions as there are emotions to be processed. Each child's needs will be different. Some kids need time to talk more frequently, others rarely. You know your children well. Think back to how they've dealt with other stressful events in their lives, and be guided by these experiences. This will be a bumpy ride, but you will get through it.

Divorce is painful for everyone, but it can also be life affirming and enriching. In the stress and tension surrounding the divorce, don't lose sight of this. One idea to model and emphasize for your children is that change is inevitable—it's part of life. Help your kids keep their perspective by reminding them that they have much to look forward to and that life will get better for them—and for you—with the passage of time. Changes, especially big ones, can be threatening to everyone involved, especially children. On the other hand, they also can be exhilarating. Life is an adventure, and it can be exciting to set forth on uncharted seas. It's appropriate and helpful to see big changes as chances for new adventures. Your children are likely to worry less and play more if they see you as someone willing to accept the changes and get on with the adventures.

Words you might use

Throughout this book we suggest language you might use for your conversations with your children. These words are examples, and may not always cover the exact situation of your family. Think of these ideas as conversation-starters that you can use as a springboard as you plan and begin your discussions. In talking with your kids, you may also find "A divorce glossary" (pages 109–111) a helpful reference.

You might start by saying:

> "We have something very important to tell you. Dad and Mom aren't going to live together anymore. We're getting a divorce. We want you to know that we both love you and are going to take good care of you. You'll always have us, and you'll always have your sisters and brothers and your friends.
>
> "We especially want you to know that we're not breaking up because of anything you said or did. You are the best thing that ever happened to us, and we will always love you.
>
> "Both of us are very sad about the divorce. You probably have lots of feelings and questions, and we can talk together about them now or later, whichever you want. Anytime you feel like talking, please let us know."

You might ask:

"What do you know about divorce?"

"Are you wondering about something in particular? What?"

"What things are you worried about?"

"What are you feeling? It's okay to talk with us about how you feel."

Your children might wonder:	*You might respond:*
"Where will I live? Who'll take care of me?"	"Mom and Dad are going to be living in two different places. You'll be spending time with both of us. Mom will take care of you when you're living with her, and Dad will take care of you when you're with him."
"Why can't you stay together?"	"We talked a lot with a counselor and we just couldn't work things out. When grown-ups can't get along, it doesn't work to stay married."

Your children might wonder:	*You might respond:*
"Will this be like the divorce that happened in my friend Jennie's family?"	"Every family's divorce is different. Jennie's father moved to another state, but your dad's staying here. What other things happened with Jennie's family's divorce?" *(This question allows you to find out what, specifically, your child is worried about.)*

"It's not your fault"

It is *never* children's fault that their parents are breaking up, but many children believe it is. When parents divorce, children often feel that they are somehow to blame. A child might think:

- "If my dad left, it must be because of something I did."
- "If Mom wants to move out, I must be unlovable."
- "I didn't clean up after myself enough."
- "I was too noisy."
- "My parents always argue when I'm around, so the divorce must be because of me."
- "It must be my fault, because Dad and Mom fought about me, and they still do."

To you these kinds of thoughts may not seem logical, but children often worry—or actually believe—that they are true. Kids rarely say these things out loud, but you can be sure they're thinking them.

Don't wait for kids to ask

Don't wait for your kids to ask, "Is the divorce because of me?" Tell children directly that the divorce is *not* their fault. Keep reassuring and reminding them frequently that the grown-ups are divorcing because of problems between themselves.

Also let your children know that neither you nor the other parent is to blame for the divorce. Even if this is something you don't agree with in your heart, it's imperative that your child not see or feel that you blame your ex-spouse for your breakup. If a child believes there's blame to assign, she'll most likely think she needs to choose sides, or feel torn because she loves the parent you seem to hold at fault. The message your child needs to hear, regularly and clearly, is this: Divorce is a grown-up solution to a grown-up problem. Nothing your child said, thought, wished, did—or *didn't* do—caused the divorce.

Keep arguments private

When parents argue in front of their children, the issue gets more complicated. Even if the argument isn't about child-related issues, kids usually feel that they're causing the fighting and therefore caused the divorce. This can negate the many "It's not your fault" statements you've made to your children, sending a mixed message. Do all that you can to keep from fighting in front of the kids. If the other parent tries to get into a discussion with you and you think things will get heated, simply say in a neutral voice, "Let's talk about this together later. I'll get in touch with you, and we can set up a time." Then follow through and make the promised contact. These discussions can be in writing if you're more comfortable communicating with your ex-spouse in that fashion. If dialogue feels impossible, consider meeting with a counselor or a mediator who could help you find strategies for cooperating with each other. You might ask your lawyer, friend, doctor, or member of the clergy to suggest someone to work with you.

What if you and your ex *do* "have words"?

If you do argue with the other parent in the children's presence, be certain to reassure your kids afterward that it was not because of them or anything they did. You might say: "I'm sorry that Mom and I had that argument in front of you. We sometimes get angry with each other, but we *weren't* angry at you." Children need stability and one way you can provide it is to demonstrate calmness after an emotional outburst that they witnessed or overheard.

It will take a long time before most children have the emotional maturity to understand the many complicated and often subtle reasons for their parents' divorce. In the meantime, they'll struggle in their own way to make sense of it, often returning to the idea that they somehow might have caused the breakup. Keep reassuring your children, and do your best not to put them in the middle of a blame game between you and your ex.

Words you might use

You might start by saying:

"I know we've talked about this before, but it's very important for you to know that the divorce is *not* your fault. Sometimes kids think that if they'd only done something different, then Mom and Dad would still be together. That's just not how it is. Nothing you did caused us to get a divorce. We had problems living together that weren't about you at all. They were grown-up problems and getting a divorce was the way we chose to solve those problems."

"Mom and I love you just the way you are—you're very special to us. Even though we aren't living together anymore, you kids are the best thing that ever happened to either one of us."

"I'm sorry that Dad and I got into that argument in front of you. We were arguing about our own problems, and we shouldn't do that in front of you. You must have felt like we were tugging you in two different directions. We both love you and we don't want you to be in the middle of our disagreements. We'll try not to let it happen again."

You might ask:

"Are you worried that we're getting divorced because of you? Let's talk about that."

"What makes you think the divorce is your fault?"

"Are you feeling torn or stuck in the middle? Can you tell me why?"

Your children might wonder:	*You might respond:*
"If it's not my fault, why were you fighting about me?"	"We don't always agree on how to handle issues about things like your schoolwork or rules you should follow. We were arguing about those ideas—not about you. You *didn't* cause our argument and the divorce isn't because of anything you said or did. We're sorry we argued in front of you."

Your children might wonder:	*You might respond:*
"Is the divorce Mom's fault?"	"The divorce isn't anybody's fault. Even if I seem mad at your mom, that doesn't mean she caused the divorce by herself. Some things about Mom upset me. Some things about me upset Mom. When married people have problems, it's not one person's fault. But the problems do make us both feel very bad."
"Why don't you try to get along like you tell us kids to do?"	"We tell you kids to talk about your problems and work to solve them together. We talked and talked about *our* problems, and the divorce is the solution we decided on."

"We will always love you"

When children learn that their parents no longer love each other and can't live together anymore, one of their most immediate fears is that Dad and Mom will stop loving *them,* too. This is a natural response. Our greatest emotional needs as human beings are love, belonging, appreciation, and approval. Our greatest fears are rejection and abandonment. Children need to be reassured that you aren't divorcing *them,* that you won't abandon them or stop loving them. Tell your children that you will always love them. Repeat this as frequently as possible. Though it's a message all children should hear often, children whose parents are divorced cannot hear it often enough.

Resist the temptation to disappear

It can happen, especially immediately after the separation, that it feels too painful for a parent to see the children. Particularly if you feel extremely hurt by or antagonistic toward the other parent, you might be tempted to stop seeing your children for a time. Resist this urge. Even though "checking out" might help you adjust, such a move can be devastating to children.

If you're in a situation where you're unable to see your kids for some time, stay in touch with them. Call, write, and email them. Let them know as often as possible that you love them and that your absence is neither their fault nor your desire. In addition to telling your children that you love them, it's important that you see your children regularly and involve yourself in their school activities, holidays, and daily lives.

If you *did* disappear from your kids' lives for a while, or didn't stay consistently involved over a period of time, forgive yourself. Tell your children that you're sorry, and resolve to stay more closely connected from here on. It's never too late to make a change for the better.

What if your ex-spouse leaves the scene, and you're in the position of having to explain the absence to your children? Tell them that the other parent loves them very much but, for grown-up reasons, she or he just can't see them right now. You don't need to make excuses for an absent parent, but you do want to comfort your kids and reassure them that they are not the reason for the absence. Even if you believe your ex-spouse is woefully self-centered, irresponsible, or inadequate as a parent, always keep in mind that a child's well-being is greatly enhanced by having as good a relationship as possible with both parents.

If the other parent has abandoned the children

It's natural for all children whose parents divorce to worry that their parents will stop loving them. When a parent has abandoned the children, this worry is more profound and intense. Your children's other parent may have walked out of their lives, or may be in touch occasionally but still basically unavailable. If this is true for your family, here's what your kids need to know and hear:

- They did not cause the other parent to go away, and *you* will always love them.

- They can talk with you and others about their loss, fears, and feelings.

- You want them to still love their other parent.

- The parent who left isn't doing the right thing, but this *doesn't* mean he or she doesn't love them.

- There are other adults besides you (grandparents, aunts and uncles, family friends) who love them, support them, and are willing to help them.

Experts recommend counseling for children who have been abandoned. If you are seeing a counselor, ask that person to recommend a therapist for your child. Otherwise, ask a social worker, lawyer, pediatrician, or member of the clergy for a referral.

When a new adult comes on the scene

New relationships parents form can threaten a child's sense of stability, causing worries to resurface or intensify. If you are dating or living with a new spouse or friend, your children may fear they're being replaced by someone else. Your kids will more easily accept such new relationships if they're confident that their place in your life is not threatened. You can demonstrate that to them by:

- continuing to tell them you will always love them

- staying involved in their activities and keeping them involved in some of yours

Words you might use

You might start by saying:

"Your dad and I got a divorce because it was the best thing for us to live apart. Even so, we both will always love you. Grown-ups sometimes fall out of love with each other, but parents don't stop loving their kids, and we won't stop loving you."

"We will never stop loving you. Our marriage is over, but being your parents is forever—and we're glad about that part."

You might start by saying:

"I know you miss Mom and don't understand why she left, but it's not your fault she went away. Sometimes grown-ups get very worried about their own problems and do things that don't make sense—like go away from their children. I hope someday Mom realizes how much you want to hear from her and see her. No matter what, I love you with all my heart and I will always be here for you."

Your children might wonder:

"You stopped loving each other, so why wouldn't you stop loving me, too?"

You might respond:

"There are many different kinds of love, and the love parents have for children is the strongest kind. Nothing you could do or say will make us stop loving you."

Your children might wonder:	*You might respond:*
"If Dad's leaving, will you leave, too, Mommy?"	"Dad's leaving because he and I decided we couldn't live together anymore. One of us has to leave, and that's going to be Dad. Even though he'll be living somewhere else, you'll get to be with him, too. You'll stay with him some of the time, and you'll talk on the phone and write letters to each other. I will stay here all the time, and when you're not with Dad, you'll stay here with me."
"If Mom loves me, why did she leave without saying goodbye? Why can't I see her or talk to her? Why doesn't she call me?"	"Mom has problems, and these problems make her forget about how wonderful you are and how much she's missing by not seeing or calling you. I know you feel sad about this, and I'm sorry about it. I want you to know that I'm here for you. I love you, and so do Nana, and Grandpa, and Grandma Kate, and Aunt Cleo, and Uncle Trahn, and Joel."*

---

* This response is adapted from *Helping Your Kids Cope with Divorce the Sandcastles Way* by M. Gary Neuman with Patricia Romanowski (New York: Times Books, 1998), page 259.

"We won't get back together"

Expect to deal again and again with children's reconciliation fantasies.

Most children of divorced parents want their dad and mom to reunite. Their happiest fantasy is for their parents to again share one home and for the family be together again. Children don't think about divorce the way adults do—they don't see it as a solution to adult problems. Instead, they cling tenaciously to their hope that the divorce will go away and that Mom and Dad will be married to each other again. Even if their parents have married other people, children of all ages are still likely to hope for a reconciliation (or hope that all the adults, stepparents included, will decide to live together).

Many kids believe a reconciliation will occur

Younger children may not be able to distinguish their desires from reality, and so the more they wish their parents would reunite, the more they start to believe it will happen. Since children readily think that the divorce might be their fault ("Daddy and Mommy divorced because I was bad"), it follows that they also easily conclude they can get their parents back together by "being good." Often children expend a great deal of time and energy imagining and attempting ways to reunite their parents. For example, if a child becomes ill or gets in trouble at school, his parents may temporarily connect in an effort to deal with the illness or problem. Seeing this, the child might decide that getting sick or having problems at school will bring his parents together again. The result might well be more illnesses or misbehavior so Mom and Dad will be together more.

Carefully monitor the messages you send

You and your ex-spouse may decide to do some things together (for example, go to a movie or have a meal as a family). If so, be aware that children are likely to interpret these actions as signs that a reconciliation is in the works. Be careful about giving mixed messages, and make it a point to tell your kids specifically that even though the family is doing certain activities together, the two of you are still divorced and this isn't going to change.

What if you and the other parent are actually thinking about getting back together? In this case, don't let the children know about it until you're absolutely sure about the decision. Even if you're feeling hopeful and excited, don't lose sight of the emotional trauma your children have been through and the new struggle they'll face if they look forward to a reconciliation that doesn't materialize. Your kids will experience a dream come true (their parents getting back together), only to be plunged once again into their worst nightmare (divorce).

It's not uncommon for one parent to want and push for a reconciliation, but it's important to recognize that this decision must be a mutual one. Painful though it may be to the parent who wants to give the marriage another chance, if the ex-spouse doesn't want to reconcile, it won't happen. In a situation like this, it's important not to talk with or in front of your kids about the possibility of getting back together. Be careful not to convey false hopes to them. True or not, a message to your children such as, "I want us to be a family, but Daddy doesn't," is the last thing they should be told. Hearing this, children will perceive that you're blaming the other parent for the divorce and your own unhappiness—and may then return to worrying about who's to blame and whether the divorce was their fault.

Words you might use

You might start by saying:

"I guess you'd like it if Dad and Mom remarried and we were all living together again. But that's not going to happen. We're divorced now and living in two different places. We worked really hard before we decided to divorce, and that decision is final."

"Sometimes I feel sad that we're divorced and won't live together ever again, and I know you do, too. I think your mom feels sad about it also, but that's just the way it is and none of us can change it."

You might ask:

"Do you understand that Mommy and Daddy won't get back together? What do you think about that?"

"Are you trying to figure out ways we can all live together again? Please tell me what you're thinking."

"What are some *good* things about the divorce?"

Your children might wonder:	*You might respond:*
"Marco's parents were going to get a divorce, but then they didn't. Maybe that will happen to us."	"Sometimes a couple separates for a time. They try living apart and then maybe decide they don't want a divorce. That's not how it is for us. Mom and I talked about our problems and decided for sure that the divorce was best for everyone. We aren't going to change our minds."

Your children might wonder:	*You might respond:*
"If I'm extra-good, will you get back together?"	"We got divorced because of our own problems. You didn't cause the divorce, and there's nothing you can do to change it. We both love you just the way you are, and we always will, even though we're divorced."
"Dad says if it was up to him, you'd still be married. So why won't you let Dad come back home?"	"Your dad and I tried to make our marriage work, but it didn't. We both wish things were different. We have grown-up problems, just between Dad and me. I know it's hard to understand, but it's important for you to know that we won't be getting back together."

"You can talk about your feelings"

Reassure children that their feelings are okay and that they are not alone. Give them ways to express and deal with feelings.

Most children weather divorces in predictable ways. Your children will experience many of the same emotions you will about the breakup—confusion, fear, stress, anger, frustration, anxiety, sadness, and hurt. Just as you will go through a grieving process, so will they.

Tune in to children's feelings

It's important to monitor your children's grieving process. The best way for anyone to grieve, adult or child, is to acknowledge, express, and release feelings—and talking about emotions is one way children can do these things. If you don't encourage and allow your children to *talk* about their feelings, it's likely that they will *act* on them. Too often, the actions will be harmful.

When a divorce happens, many children, especially younger ones, may regress into an earlier developmental stage. This usually isn't a matter for too much concern unless it lasts a long time or is unusually severe. ("Resources for you and your family," pages 112–119, includes books with information on child development.) Major and lingering changes in behavior, however, are signs that your child may be having serious adjustment problems. Sudden declines, as well as sudden increases, in grades are one such sign. Significant personality shifts are another. New and undesirable friends are also a warning flag. While emotions such as anger and sadness are to be expected, some children will exhibit ongoing, intense emotions, and this is a concern. Some kids will withdraw; others may cry excessively or demonstrate extreme anger. If you see such signs or others that trouble you, talk with your former spouse and get professional help for your child as well as advice about how *you* can help. If your child has been abused physically or emotionally by the other parent or has witnessed abuse in the parents' relationship, it's particularly important that you seek professional counseling and guidance.

The formal processes of divorce can, in themselves, lead children to feel anxious and scared. Getting divorced usually involves attorneys and going to court, even if just for the purpose of having documents signed. If you're going to be working with attorneys, mediators, or custody evaluators, tell your children something about what's going on. It is not unusual for children to have to speak with court-appointed experts or judges during the process. In addition, children tend to listen in on conversations their parents have with attorneys or others about a divorce. Professionals working with children during a divorce report that when they talk to children the first time, these boys and girls often have no idea what's going on or why they're talking to someone. Children can become frightened and fear that they might be taken away from one of their parents. Just as you prepare your children for a visit to the doctor's office, you'll want to reassure them about the court process and let them know what to expect. Tell them that you're working with these professionals or with a judge to help you come up with the best plan for everybody in the family. If they'll be talking to a specialist regarding custody or a time-sharing schedule, explain that they will meet and speak with someone, but that they will not be asked to choose between Dad and Mom.

For some children, there is a sense of relief about the divorce. Relief might come for a child whose parents argued often or whose home atmosphere before the divorce was extremely tense, angry, or unhappy. If a parent had problems with alcohol or other drugs or was physically or emotionally abusive, a child might begin to feel relieved when the tension and fear subside. Some children are confused or guilty about feeling this way. If you suspect a child is relieved, let her know that it's okay to feel relief and hope for a better future.

Grieving vs. warning signs of adjustment problems[*]

A child mourning the end of a marriage may experience a range of emotions and behaviors, including:	A child who is having difficulty adjusting may show exaggerated responses and other warning signs, such as:
changes in sleeping patterns	inability to sleep at all, sleeping constantly, frequent nightmares
some health problems	ongoing health problems such as headaches or stomach-aches, extended changes in eating habits, significant weight loss or gain
guilt	intense self-blame, attempts at being perfect

anger	explosive behavior, destructiveness, purposely hurting self or others, school troubles, lying, stealing
sadness	withdrawing to the point of isolation, giving away personal possessions, crying excessively, or expressing deep despair
clinging to or withdrawing from friends to some degree	rejecting old friends and forming friendships that parents find atypical and/or undesirable
developmental regression (behaving like a younger child)	significant changes in personality, running away from home or childcare setting
acceptance of the divorce	refusal to accept the divorce

If your daughter or son is experiencing warning signs of adjustment problems, it's critical that you seek professional help for the child. Share your concerns with your ex-spouse and consult with a psychologist, counselor, or medical professional right away.

* Adapted from *Children of Divorce in School-Age Care* by Carole D. Weisberg (Nashville, TN: School-Age NOTES, 2000), pages 13 and 24. Used by permission.

Help children talk about their feelings

Encourage your children to talk about their feelings, whatever they are. Do what you can to make it safe for them to do this, even if you're afraid that they'll say things that will be hurtful to you. For example, if you see behavior that indicates anger, tell your child it's normal to feel angry and that it's okay to tell you about it. Sometimes parents judge children's emotions and say things like, "You don't need to be angry" or "Now don't get mad about this." The problem with this type of response is that children conclude their feelings are "bad" or "wrong." They might respond by feeling guilty, trying to deny or bury the feelings, or acting out. Don't judge your kids' emotions. Emotions simply are. Grief comes. Anger happens. Sadness is a part of divorce. Fear is normal. Stress and anxiety are to be expected.

Watch your facial expressions as well as your words when you talk to your children about their feelings. Try not to smile if one of your children says something negative about your ex-spouse that gives you a moment of pleasure. Avoid the urge to frown when a child mentions something positive about your ex. Your kids love you both. They need you both. They need you to make it safe for them to share their emotions. *You* are the one who can help them now. Take heart in the knowledge that your children feel secure enough with you to express those feelings.

Some children do not easily share or discuss their feelings. Others may go through developmental stages during which they don't want to talk about their feelings, at least with their parents. "How are you feeling?" may be greeted with little more than a grunt of "Fine." It can be difficult to get beyond these one-syllable responses, but it's important to try. Sometimes we parents simply miss clues and signals that our children give us. "Fine" can mean that the child is in fact doing all right and simply isn't feeling talkative. It can also be a kind of mechanical response hiding the fact that a child is struggling and doesn't know how to talk about it. There are no firm and fast guidelines here. Do your best to evaluate all the evidence available to you, constantly being open to the possibility that your child is hurting and needs help.

Ask open questions

In encouraging children to talk about their feelings, open questions are more effective than closed ones. A closed question suggests a yes-or-no reply and nothing more: "Are you feeling confused?" "Is something worrying you?" "Do you feel sad?" Open questions invite children to tell you what they're thinking and feeling. The easiest way to ask an open question is to begin with "How," "What," or "Why": "How are you feeling?" "What's going on inside you?" "Why do you think it's hard to talk about it?"

Open questions don't imply that there's a right or wrong answer; they give no clues about what reply you would like to hear. From time to time your children *will* give you the answer they think you want from them. You're an important part of their world, and they may not want to displease you. For example, suppose you ask your child, "You look pretty upset. Are you feeling unhappy?" Maybe your child is actually feeling angry or frustrated but, hearing your question, decides that unhappiness—and not anger—is what's acceptable to you right now. Instead, you might say, "You look pretty upset. Whatever you're feeling is okay to talk about with me. Please tell me about it."

Open questions won't necessarily guarantee that children will talk freely, but they will encourage this. You'll also want to be careful not to cross-examine your children. You may need to make a few attempts, at different times and in different ways, in order to gradually learn how your kids are feeling and figure out what you can do to help.

Depending on your children's ages, you'll want to invite them to discuss their emotions about the breakup in different ways. Some seven- and even eight-year-olds can be asked indirect questions, such as, "I wonder how your Teddy bear is feeling about having to live in two places?" or, "I bet it's hard for Teddy to understand all this. How do you think we could explain it to him?"

Older children can be asked directly or indirectly. An indirect question might be, "How are your friends reacting to the news that we're getting a divorce?" A direct question might be prefaced with a comment such as, "This must be hard on you" or "This isn't much fun right now." Then ask, "What can we do to make it better?"

Encourage children to talk to others, too

It's not uncommon for a child whose parents are divorcing to think that he is the only child in the world having such a traumatic experience. These feelings of loneliness and isolation can cause a child to internalize unpleasant emotions and prevent him from talking about the experience. Remind your child that he's not alone. It's highly likely that there are other children—at school, in the neighborhood, or at your place of worship—whose parents are also divorced. Your child may not even realize this, so you may have to help him see it.

Children frequently are hesitant to discuss or even mention their parents' divorce. They often have difficulty talking about such things and may not understand what's troubling them. Think of ways to help. For instance, some schools have support groups for kids of divorce. If your child's school doesn't, consider talking to the school about starting one. Community agencies, too, may have organized groups for preteens who are going through a divorce. Many places of worship also have excellent youth groups. Often these groups welcome children regardless of whether they participate in organized religious activities. Even if the group isn't focused on divorce, your child may find support from the other kids and the leaders in this kind of structured setting.

You know each of your children better than anyone else. Do what you can to help them open up and talk about the divorce. Remind them that they're not alone. Encourage them to ask questions. Not only will your children feel better, but they may help other kids who are having similar feelings. The more that children are able to share their experience safely, the less frightened and alone they're likely to feel.

Don't be overly concerned if a child talks more about his feelings with your ex than with you. All children pass through many developmental stages, and during some of those times they may be closer to their other parent. By the age of eleven or twelve, it's natural and healthy for kids to begin to separate from parents. Because children's friends may be as important to them as you during these preteen years, they may well be discussing their feelings about the divorce with other kids their own age. Nonetheless, they are having strong emotions about the divorce and need to talk to an adult, too, whether that's you, your ex, or someone else.

If your children, for whatever reason, seem not to be sharing their emotions with you, encourage them to talk with other trusted adults. Even if they *are* completely open with you, it's still a good idea to suggest that they talk with other people they feel safe with. These might be other family adults such as grandparents or aunts and uncles, parents of friends, or a teacher, care provider, neighbor, counselor, social worker, or member of the clergy.

Other children can help as well. If your family includes more than one child, you may be amazed at how much support your kids give each other. Encourage them to talk together. Many children of divorce who are now adults report that having a sibling was one of the things that helped them most during and after the divorce. These siblings learned at an early age that other family members can be of huge assistance in weathering life's crises.

Give children other ways to deal with feelings

The most important thing for children to do is express what they're feeling. They watch you carefully, so model ways of accepting and dealing with feelings. Tell your kids that feelings, especially unpleasant ones like anger and fear, lose much of their power once they are released. Acknowledging and talking about intense feelings helps children gradually move beyond them. Here are some other ways you can help your kids deal with emotions.

1. **Physical activity.** Physical exercise is a healthy way to express and let go of strong feelings. Running, kicking or batting a ball, shooting baskets, jumping rope, or climbing on equipment at the playground are all activities that provide great emotional release. So do

dancing and movement. Slow, deep breathing is
a quieter physical outlet that also helps.

2. **Crying.** Tears are an important release for
anger, stress, frustration, and sadness. Tell
your children, boys and girls alike, that crying
can help them feel better by letting out the
feelings they have inside. Honor their tears.

3. **Drawing and writing.** Encourage children to draw or write about
their feelings as well. They may want to draw detailed pictures of
scenes or situations that are troubling to them, or paint using
colors and motions that match their mood. You might give your
child a diary or a notebook to use for journaling. Invite children
to share their drawings and writings, but also let them know that
you'll respect their privacy.

4. **Music.** Many children find music enjoyable and therapeutic. It
can be a catalyst for writing, drawing, and thinking about feelings.

5. **Quiet reflection.** Like adults, children may find it helpful at times
to just sit down and experience the emotions they have inside,
letting feelings of anger, fear, loneliness, or hurt wash over them.

6. **Laughter.** Children need to be able to talk, think about their feelings, express and understand their strong emotions, and release
them. They also need to discover through this process that things
will get better and that they will be all right. They need time for
this to happen, and they need you to remind and reassure them
that time will be part of what helps them. Through it all, don't

forget to help your kids have fun and laugh. Watching funny movies or TV shows, sharing jokes, reading humorous books or cartoons together, and just being goofy can distract kids, cheer them up, and help diffuse some of the overpowering feelings tugging at their hearts. Laughter is good for everyone—your children *and* you.

When talking makes things worse

For some kids, the more they talk about their feelings concerning the breakup, the more upset they get. Occasionally parents may press a child to talk and find that the child becomes nearly hysterical. When children are routinely overanxious and obsessive about the divorce, talking about it may need to wait. What can you do for children in this situation? Acknowledge their intense feelings. Help them develop strategies to distract and calm themselves. When they start to feel overwhelmed by their emotions, children might read a favorite book, watch a funny TV show, play a game, or do some other activity that will ease stress and refocus their thoughts.

It's possible that some children won't be ready to discuss their feelings for a long time. Use your own instincts and knowledge of your child to decide when and how to encourage talking about feelings. If your daughter or son continues to have serious difficulties coping, consult a social worker, counselor, or specialist at school.

Words you might use

You might start by saying:

"The divorce is hard for all of us. Some days I feel sad, and other times I feel mad. You've probably noticed me talking with Aunt Kay on the phone a lot. Talking about how I feel really helps me. I know you're feeling lots of things, too. Whatever you're feeling is okay. You can talk to me about your feelings whenever you want to."

"Sometimes it must feel like you're the only person around whose parents are divorced, but you're not. There are other kids at school who have divorced parents and live in two places just like you. Your teacher told me there's a group of kids who get together each week to talk about their parents' divorce. The counselor's going to tell you about it soon."

You might ask:

"How are you feeling?"

"What are you thinking about?"

"I haven't seen you smiling much lately. What could we do to help you feel better?"

You might ask:

"I think most kids whose parents are divorcing might feel pretty worried about what's going to happen. What are *you* feeling?"

"Why do you think you feel like fighting with your sister so much right now?"

"There's been a lot of tension for a long time in our home. Now I'm feeling relieved. How about you?"

"Would you like to try to make friends with some other kids whose parents are divorcing?"

"I'd like to do something fun together. What could we do?"

Your children might wonder:

"Is it wrong for me to be mad at Daddy?"

You might respond:

"It's not wrong to feel mad. Feelings aren't good or bad, they just are. It's a good idea to talk to Daddy about how you're feeling."

Your children might wonder:	*You might respond:*
"Why can't I see Mom today?"	"I know you miss your mom and wish you could see her before the weekend. What are you looking forward to doing with her?" *(You might encourage your child to draw a picture or write a story about what she misses or looks forward to.)* "Would you like to call her and tell her you're thinking about her?"
"Why do I feel so bad all the time?"	"The divorce is hard in lots of ways, and it brings lots of hard feelings. Please tell me about your bad feelings."
"How could you and Mom do this to me? I hate you both!"	"You're angry about the divorce, and I understand that. I'd be angry, too, if I were you. Even though you feel like you hate us, we still love you very much." *(You might want to arrange for your child to talk to another adult about the angry feelings.)*

"Here's how we'll be living"

Make the most humane living arrangements possible for your children.

Children think concretely. When their parents divorce, children's worries are very basic: "Will there be enough to eat?" "Will I still have my room?" "Where will I keep my toys?" "When will I see Dad?" "Will Mom still come to my soccer games?" As you move forward making changes in living arrangements, you'll want to reassure your children about these kinds of concerns frequently—whether children ask you directly about them or not.

Living in two homes is stressful. There's confusion about which clothes are at what place, where homework has been left, how to connect with friends and get to activities, and what's happening day to day. This often doesn't get easier for kids with the passage of time. In fact, many preteens and teens eventually express a desire for dual-home living arrangements to stop. This is seldom a reflection on either parent, but simply a weariness with all the back and forth.

If you have any doubt that living in two homes is stressful, you and the other parent might try a living situation called *bird-nesting*. This is where the children live in one home and the parents take turns moving in and out. Courts occasionally order this kind of arrangement on an interim basis during the resolution of legal issues. Many parents quickly come to hate living this way, but it gives them a good idea of what their children experience going from one home to another and can sometimes help the parents decide on the most compassionate time-sharing plans possible for their children.

Consider what's best for your children

There are all kinds of living arrangements divorced parents make for their children, and there's no right or wrong way to set these up. What works for one child may be totally unworkable for another. This chapter offers some general guidelines for time-sharing arrangements.

In planning living arrangements, it's important take into account each child's particular temperament, age, maturity, and needs. If you have more than one child, different schedules might work better for each one. Even though it's best in most cases not to separate the children from one another, you may want to create individualized "special times"—days or evenings for each child to be alone with one parent while the siblings are with the other. This kind of arrangement can be particularly helpful for a child needing extra attention from one or both of the parents.

If you and the other parent are having trouble deciding what's best for your children, consult a mental health professional or family counselor to give you guidance. There are also professional mediators who are trained in helping families reach agreements during divorces, including decisions about children's living arrangements. Usually, mediators are far less expensive than lawyers, work much faster, and provide greater satisfaction. Divorcing couples who successfully mediate all or part of their divorces, as opposed to litigating them in the courts, often have less future conflict and quieter relationships, which is always better for the kids. Check with the court or a social worker for a referral, or look in the Yellow Pages under Mediation Service.

Eventually, if you cannot agree on what's best for your children, a judge will decide for you. This is rarely the best way to resolve the issue. It is not a good idea for the two of you to abdicate the responsibility for deciding your own time-sharing arrangement. You know your children far better than anyone else. The more you can agree on, the better your divorce and subsequent contacts will be—and the better your children's lives will be.

Moving is a very big deal for children

As you plan how you and your children will be living, keep in mind that avoiding a full-blown move is desirable if at all possible. Having a parent move far away is upsetting and frightening to most children. Still, whether you or your ex-partner will move a couple of doors down the block, a few miles away, or to an entirely new community, your children will experience some kind of move. Along with the many other adjustments of divorce, moving will give your children yet another change to navigate. A move can be a serious blow to a child's security. It's best if you and your ex talk to your kids together about the move. Don't take this conversation lightly. Share with your children the reasons that make the move necessary. Let them know far in advance about the move and make it clear that you'll do as much as you can to ease the transition for them.

Involve your children in the move; make it an adventure:

- Several weeks ahead of the move, begin talking about it. Ask children what questions they have, and answer honestly and reassuringly. When there's a choice your children can make—about what color to paint their rooms or which games and books should come along—invite them to make it.

- Throughout the planning and after the move, talk often with your kids about what things *won't* change and *haven't* changed: You're still a family. You will always love each other. Your kids will still have certain important possessions, enjoy favorite activities, and eat familiar foods.

- If possible, take children to see their new home ahead of time. Explore the new neighborhood together. If children can't see the home before the move, show them pictures of it and of other areas in the new community.

- Help children put together individual boxes or backpacks of important belongings that they'll want to have with them right after the move.

- Keep children feeling stable and secure with plenty of hugs and as much routine as possible. Arrange for extended family to be with you and your children if you can—this provides support and reassurance to everyone.

All of these different actions give children the important message that they will be okay.

What about a new school and new friends?

School is a child's home away from home. For older kids, school is their world. A new school means getting used to new teachers, rules, classmates, and activities. It means making new friends and finding a place in this new world. Both the "job" of schoolwork and the connections to familiar, comfortable friends are altered when a child begins a new school. On top of the trauma of divorce and the many other changes that come with it, switching to a new school can be extremely difficult, even overwhelming. For all these reasons, we urge you to do everything within your power not to transfer your children to a new school. If that's not possible, help your child adjust to a new school by keeping these guidelines in mind:

- Be upbeat but honest in talking to your child about finding new friends. Tell him it will take time and may not be easy, but that you know he'll gradually make friends.

- Ask the new teacher to suggest kids your child might get along with; then arrange some activities or outings for the children to get acquainted.

- Encourage your child to sign up for activities so he'll meet other kids who share similar interests.

- Welcome new friends into your home.

- Support your child in staying in touch with old friends.

Guidelines for making back-and-forth living easier

There is a great deal you can do to make it easier for your children to go back and forth between two homes. Here are a few ideas. We encourage you to think of others.

1. **Work out a time-sharing arrangement that does not involve too many transitions.** If you and the other parent have an equal time-sharing schedule, there are many ways to minimize transitions. An alternating-week schedule, for example, has far fewer transitions than alternating days. Time-sharing plans need to be based on each child's developmental stage and maturity level. The schedule will need adjustments as your kids grow older. Older children and adults whose parents were divorced frequently report that one of the most frustrating and unpleasant aspects of the divorce was what they perceived as a lack of input and choice about their time-sharing arrangements. Pages 62–64 discuss ways to make transitions easier.

2. **Make sure your kids *play*.** You can help your children a great deal by seeing to it that they stay in touch and play with their important friends. Though this may involve lots of transportation obligations for you, it's worth it. Make it a priority to help your child form new social connections as well, so there'll be friends to spend time with in both homes. If your child has a favorite pet, consider the same time-sharing schedule for the pet. Pets can help a lot during a divorce.

3. **Focus often on what's fun about living in two homes.** The differences between two homes can mean "pluses" for each. Perhaps a child likes her bedroom more in one home, but enjoys the park next to her other home. Maybe it's fun to be with kids from the familiar neighborhood, but also fun to explore a new library. Many children, too, relish the idea of two birthday parties, two Halloweens, two holiday occasions, and two summer vacations. They will have special time with each parent now.

4. **Help children keep their own calendar with their schedule on it.** This gives kids a positive and real sense of control. They can consult their calendar and tell their friends where they will be when. They can check to see who'll pick them up after school. A calendar lets children *see* when they'll be with the other parent, even if it's only for holidays or during the summer. A calendar is a concrete tool that eases confusion and increases a child's sense of structure and stability. Give your children calendars and help them keep these planners up to date. If you and the other parent haven't yet worked out a schedule for the kids, tell them that you will be doing so. As much as possible, keep their daily routines the same. Explain to your children that they need to help remember some things, too, and that they'll have to make an effort to stay organized.

5. **Deliver suitcases and backpacks to the other parent's home on transition days.** It can be embarrassing for children to have to take a suitcase or backpack full of clothes to school with them.

6. **Communicate with the other parent about school issues.** Do this so the burden is not on your kids to remember to tell both parents everything about homework and school events. If verbal communication is difficult, do it in writing or by email. Don't use your children to communicate with your ex. (For more on this topic, see pages 91–93.)

7. **Ask teachers to send copies of school notices to both homes.** Give teachers a set of self-addressed, stamped envelopes for this purpose. Be open about this change in your family. Request that teachers contact both you and the other parent if they see signs of adjustment difficulties such as fatigue, anger, withdrawal, or behavior changes.

8. **Be willing to change your child's schedule if he appears to have difficulty with it.** Sometimes children are so stressed as a result of their schedules that they can't put energy into their schoolwork or into playing and having fun. However, be alert to the possibility that the schedule isn't a serious problem and you are simply being manipulated. To assess this, listen to your child, ask his other parent how the arrangement seems to be going for him, take into account what you know about his personality and needs, and make your best judgment.

9. **Be on time to pick up your children. Make it a personal rule to never be late.** Your kids need to know they're important enough to you for you to be on time. Also know that being late can trigger abandonment fears in children. If you're running unavoidably behind, get word to your children somehow. Call them directly or have a trusted adult let them know that you've been delayed but will be there soon.

10. **Prepare your children for trips if they will travel long distances to see the other parent.** Remember that it can be frightening to get on an airplane, train, or bus alone. Make careful and thorough plans for any traveling children will do on their own. Call the transportation company and arrange for an adult to accompany your children. Check into the airline's rules and chaperoning procedures. Try to plan nonstop air travel; if connecting flights are necessary, allow time between flights and make sure children know how to find the flight they need and what adult will help them. When children are traveling, be available to them by phone at any time.

Words you might use

You might start by saying:

"With the divorce, you'll live with me some of the time and with Mom some of the time. We'll have to get two homes organized. It may be messy and hard for a while, but Mom and I will do all we can to keep life going smoothly. You can help us decide what things you want to have at both homes. Some of the things we'll take back and forth, some you can leave at Mom's, and some you can leave at my place. This will be a big change for us, but we'll make it work."

"Dad and I have to tell you some news: I'm going to be moving to a new town. You'll live here with Dad a lot of the time, and you'll go to school here, but you'll live with me during summer and some vacations. I have to move because of my job, and I wish I didn't have to. We both want you to understand that I am *not* leaving you. Besides the times you stay with me, we'll talk together and write each other letters. I'm moving next month, and you'll come see me as soon as school is out. Even though Dad and I will be living in two different towns, we'll still take care of you and we'll talk to each other about the things you need, just like we do now. We'll always love you and we'll always take care of you."

You might ask:

"What questions do you have about living in two homes?"

"Are you worried about how all this will work for you? What are you wondering about?"

"What do you want to know about the new town I'm moving to?"

"What do you think will be different about having two homes? What will stay the same? What do you think will be fun about these changes?"

Your children might wonder:	*You might respond:*
"How will I practice the piano at Dad's apartment?" "What bus will I take from school to Daddy's new house?" "What if I forget my medicine at Mom's?"	*(Be prepared to answer specific questions like these that relate to your children's needs and situation.)*
"How will I see my friends when I'm at Mommy's?"	"Your friends can come play when you're at Mommy's home, too. We'll talk to their parents and figure out rides for them."

Your children might wonder:	*You might respond:*
"Why do you have to move so far away?"	"I was transferred because of my job. Right now I can't find a different job, so I have to move. But we'll talk on the phone and email a lot. You'll come visit me, and I'll visit you, too."
"What will I do when I visit you? How will I find friends?"	"You'll still be going to school here and you'll get to keep your friends here. And when you come to see me, I'll make sure we find some friends for you there, too."

"We'll help make it easier"

Provide as much structure and consistency as possible.

One ten-year-old we know said to us, "I don't like having two different pillows." This is a telling statement about what it's like for a child to live in two homes. No matter how much your children love you and want to be with both parents, going back and forth from one home to the other will be difficult for them. This is especially true at transition times. Transitions between two homes are hard on everyone, children and grown-ups alike.

Tips for making transitions easier

There are a number of ways you can make switching from one home to the other easier for your children—and ultimately easier for you as well. Here are some suggestions.

1. **Drive or accompany your kids to the other parent's home.** It's usually best when the parent the children are leaving delivers them to the "receiving" parent. This eases the transition for the children by demonstrating to them that the receiving parent isn't the cause of any disappointment they may feel at leaving their other parent.

2. **Transitions may be easier if they occur on school days.** For many families, it works well when the parent who the children

are leaving takes them to school and the receiving parent picks them up at the end of the day. The switch occurs at school in an environment kids are used to and they don't have to watch any parental interactions.

3. **Let your words and attitude show that time spent with the other parent is a positive thing.** Keep your tears from your children at transition times. If you cry or look sad and tell them how much you'll miss them, they'll feel torn. It can be heartbreaking for you to drop your children off and then leave. Painful as this is, keep in mind what your children need from you. The confidence and positive attitude you show tells them that you want them to love and spend time with their other parent and to be happy while they're in the other home. If they see that you're hurt or unhappy, this message won't come through. Take a deep breath and put on a normal face. Save your tears until you're away from your children. Give them a kiss and a hug; say that you'll be fine while they're gone, that you want them to have a good time, and that you'll look forward to when they come back. This is a practical way for you to show them that you don't need them to be your caretaker. The message you send is, "I am the adult. I can take care of myself, and I'll take care of you."

4. **Tell your kids you love them, and let them know when they'll hear from you again.** You'll need to be the judge of whether it's best to call later the same day or wait until the next day. You may be longing to call, but choose the time to do it

based on what you think is best for your kids. The younger they are, the more likely it is that a call from you will be reassuring. Even then, you'll want to wait several hours until they've had a chance to settle into their other home. Older children generally don't need as much reassurance and may even resent a phone call from you on the first day.

5. **After you leave, try to do something nice for yourself.** You might treat yourself to a cup of coffee, visit a friend, watch a movie, find a quiet place to have a good cry, or go home and put on some music you like. Indulge in the break from parenting.

6. **When the children return to your home, give them time to readjust.** As the kids go through this reentry process, let them have some quiet time before you start activities. Be guided by your children. If they're clingy or following you around, they probably don't want to be left alone. On the other hand, remoteness may be a clue that they need a little time to ease back into the environment. Imagine that each transition is like a bridge. Give your kids time to walk across.

When a child begs not to go*

One of the most frequent concerns divorced parents express in custody disputes is that when their child is supposed to spend time with the

---

* The material in "When a child begs not to go," pages 64–66, is adapted from "A Child Cries, A Parent Misinterprets" by the Honorable Anne Kass, a family court judge in Albuquerque, New Mexico. Used with permission.

other parent, the child cries, clings, or begs not to have to go. The "delivering" parent generally interprets this to mean the child doesn't like to spend time with the other parent or that the other parent is incompetent, irresponsible, or even abusive.

In fact, there are many possible reasons children resist going from one parent to the other:

- The children really might not want to spend time with the other parent, sometimes with good cause. But this is actually rare. (See "If a child needs protection," page 68.)

- The children may want to spend time with the other parent but not want to leave the parent they're with.

- The children may sense nonverbal clues that the parent they're leaving is sad to have them go. When they say they don't want to go, they may actually be reflecting the parent's feelings, not their own.

- The children may believe that begging to stay pleases the parent they're leaving.

- As noted earlier, the children may find making the transition from one home to the other uncomfortable. This is usually a temporary upset. Some children welcome change. Others have a more difficult time with it.

It's wise not to jump to conclusions when a child resists leaving. If pleading not to go becomes a recurring issue, it's in everyone's best interests for you and your ex-spouse to find a counselor to help the family sort out what's troubling the child.

Just as important as figuring out the child's true concerns is finding a solution to the problem—and stopping visitation or time-sharing is rarely the best answer. The counselor can help you devise ways for your child to comfortably spend time in both homes. Often it's the parents who need to learn new skills, such as how to give their children sincere permission to feel and express love for both parents.

Transitions are among the most difficult parts of divorces. For many people, they never get any easier. But they are moments when you can show your kids just how much you do love them. There's no more profound demonstration of a parent's love than to let your children go to their other parent knowing you want this experience to be a special and important part of their lives.

When a child behaves differently in each home

Judge Anne Kass has observed and written about another situation that may arise when children live in two homes. Sometimes a child will behave like a "model" daughter or son in one parent's home, and then misbehave or act out in the other. Typically in this case, the parent who isn't having trouble assumes the other parent is doing something to bring on the misbehavior. Often, however, a child misbehaves with a parent who seems more stable or sensible. Explains Kass, "The child might think, 'It's safe for me to misbehave at this parent's home. It's safe for me to be a child here.' At the other parent's home, the child might be feeling insecure or accepting too much responsibility. The child might think, 'I need to be especially strong and good because this parent doesn't have the strength or patience to cope with my acting like a child.'" Judge Kass recommends that a divorced parent whose children misbehave at one home but not at the other seek advice from a counselor.

When the rules are different

All children need predictability and reliable structure in their lives. Children whose parents are divorced need it even more. Reasonable rules of behavior give your children the stability and security they need. Rules surrounding chores, manners, dressing, homework, bedtimes, and activities are all gifts of structure that parents give children. No matter how much whining and complaining kids may do, they know that the rules you set demonstrate that you love and care about them.

Of course, the rules in your home and in your ex-partner's won't necessarily be the same. This is okay. Children can understand and accept that rules about snacking between meals, talking on the phone, or watching TV are different in each home.

For your part, establish reasonable rules and stick to them. Usually your kids are testing you when they complain about the rules. Of course, if a particular rule seems to seriously trouble your child, be willing to talk about it and make a change if this seems helpful. What your children need is to know that you are in charge and responsible. The result of your firmness is a world that's secure and safe for them.

You won't be perfect, and there will be times when maintaining family rules is almost too much effort. Moreover, all children occasionally attempt to manipulate the rules and their parents. The divorce will give them the opportunity, which they *will* use, to try to sway or provoke you with arguments like, "I don't have to do that at Dad's" or "Mom doesn't make us do that!"

Parenting isn't a popularity contest. You may feel, rightly or wrongly, that your ex-spouse is trying to be the kids' best friend rather than their parent. You may believe there's a deliberate attempt to anger or frustrate you by being too lenient with your children. Or you may think there's too much strictness in the other home. Maybe, in fact, your ex is truly unreliable. There are people who are chronically late, disorganized, or inconsiderate. Frankly, there's not much you can do about this except ensure stability in *your* home. If your child's other parent is lax or ineffective about rules, neither you nor the courts will likely be able to change that. This means it's all the more important for you to provide predictable structure when the kids are with you. There is a kind of peace that comes when you realize what you can and can't control and when you are able to let go of the illusion that you can change the other parent's behavior or parenting style.

If a child needs protection

Sadly, there are adults who have extremely poor parenting skills or whose own problems lead them to be neglectful or even abusive toward children. If you sincerely believe your child may not be safe with the other parent, consult an attorney, a mediator, or a counselor right away. A court may arrange for supervised visitation, where the other parent sees the child in the presence of another adult both you and your ex agree to. Such arrangements are rare, but can be helpful in the case of abuse or serious neglect.

Words you might use

You might start by saying:

About an hour before time to leave: "We have to leave to take you to Dad's in about an hour. Let's make sure everything you want to take is ready to go. We don't want to forget anything."

About thirty minutes before time to leave: "We need to go in a little while. Let's save a few minutes to talk before we leave. It's time to put away the things that are staying here."

If you're meeting resistance to leaving: "It must be hard to have to leave right now. We've had a great time together, haven't we? I always like it when you're here with me. But now it is time for you to go to Dad's. I won't let us be late. I hope you have a great time with him. I know he's going to be glad to see you, and I want you to be happy while you're with him. I'll see you again on Sunday night. Don't forget that you can call me if you want."

When dropping off your child: "I love you very much, and I'll call later to say hi. I'm glad you get to be with Dad, and I want you to have a great time while you're here."

You might ask:

"What are you looking forward to doing at Dad's?"

"What's hard for you about leaving? What would make it easier?"

Your children might wonder:	*You might respond:*
"Why do I have to go? Why can't I stay here?"	"Now that we're divorced, both Mom and I need to spend time with you. She and I agreed to a schedule, and this is the weekend you go to her place."
"Will you feel bad if I have a good time at Mom's?"	"I want you to have a good time at Mom's. Even though she and I aren't married any-more, we both love you and we want you to love us both. We want you to have a good time with both of us."

Your children might wonder:	*You might respond:*
"Why are the rules different?"	"Dad and I have different ideas about rules. But we both love you, and we both *have* rules that we want you to follow. At Dad's you follow the rules for his place. Here, you follow the rules for this place."
"Why are you so strict? Mom's not."	"Rules are important. I know some of the rules are different when you're at Mom's, and that's okay. But you are with me now and this is the rule here."
"If a rule doesn't work, can't we change it?"	"Tell me what's not working for you. I'm willing to change something if I think it will be the right thing for you."

"You can love us both"

Give children genuine permission to love both parents.

Despite behavior that sometimes seems to the contrary, children want to love and please *both* their parents. They often feel tremendous loyalty conflicts after a divorce or separation. They know that you don't love their other parent anymore, so they're not certain it's okay with you if *they* continue to love him or her. You need to let them know it is. In fact, you need to give your children explicit permission to love and spend time with the other parent.

This is no easy task. It's natural for adults in a divorce to want the people around them to "take their side" in the aftermath of the breakup. Divorcing parents are often ready to tell anyone who will listen—children included—why the divorce was the other person's fault. We want our children to believe what we believe, and it can be difficult to watch them love someone we once loved but no longer do. We somehow feel rejected and scared: "If my children love my ex, does that mean they no longer love me?" This is a natural emotion that occasionally arises for many divorcing parents. Not uncommonly, parents also resent each other and enjoy hearing about the other's faults from the kids. Even if you feel this way, the most loving thing you can do for your children is encourage them to love and respect their other parent. This is true even to the extent, if necessary, of helping them accept and forgive the parent's shortcomings. That can be a tall order, especially if you feel that your former spouse fails miserably at being a parent or was the sole cause of the divorce. Yet it's what your children need from you.

Give your child permission to love the other parent

In giving your child permission to love, respect, and interact with the other parent, your actions will speak as loudly as your words. There are many ways you can encourage your child:

- When your child is missing the other parent, respect her feelings. Let her call her dad or mom if it will help her feel better. You may even want to give up or exchange this particular segment of the child's time with you. Your willingness to be flexible is a positive example not only to your child, but also to your ex.

- Let your child have pictures of the other parent in her room. A special photo album is a good way to do this.

- Show interest and happiness if your child is telling you what a good time she had at the other parent's home.

From time to time, one or the other of your children probably will announce that they hate the other parent. Such statements usually mean a child is angry at the parent. When you hear these things, keep in mind that children make these kinds of remarks in all families. In homes where parents aren't divorced, such emotions are easier to handle. The temptation for one parent to encourage a child's animosity toward the other is usually absent. Moreover, the person the child is angry at is right there, or will be soon, and can respond to the feelings and help defuse them. In divorced families this isn't the case. While it might feel good to hear your child say such things, the results of encouraging a child, even subtly, to dislike the other parent will do harm. When one parent invites disrespect toward the other, or tries to turn a child against the other parent, a day will probably come when the child resents it terribly. The adage "What goes around comes around" can be true for divorced parents. The anger that's directed toward your former spouse today might, tomorrow or years from now, be directed toward you.

Letting your children love a parent whose attitude toward you is rude and disrespectful is hard. It can feel unbearable. Unfortunately, divorce brings out the worst in some people. If this is true of your former spouse, you may feel such a mix of betrayal, hurt, anger, disappointment, sorrow, and frustration that keeping in check your own negative feelings about your ex seems impossible. Painful as this is, take a deep breath and think about what's best for your kids. If you find that your negative feelings about your former spouse are getting in the way of your parenting, think about getting some outside help, perhaps from a counselor or religious advisor. It's worth doing for your children. ("Resources for you and your family" includes two books you might find particularly helpful in this situation: *Joint Custody with a Jerk*, page 115, and *"Why Did You Have to Get a Divorce? And When Can I Get a Hamster?,"* page 116.)

One of the most difficult circumstances for giving a child permission to love the other parent is during or after a divorce that involved a serious betrayal, such as an affair. The temptation to demonize the unfaithful spouse is especially strong in such situations. So, too, is the desire to let the children know what happened so they won't blame you for the divorce. But these are adult matters, and not things children should know about.

If, in the years ahead, it does become appropriate to discuss this— and it's possible it never will—it's the job of the straying spouse to talk with the children. There will be other occasions, too, when children ask you about matters regarding the other parent that you should refer to that parent—for instance, questions about the parent's dating relationships or subsequent marriages, financial matters, or career. Gently but firmly decline to answer or speculate.

Words you might use

You might start by saying:

"Mommy and I are divorced now, but we haven't stopped loving you—and we never will. We know you won't stop loving us, either. I want you to love Mommy, and I want you to spend time with her."

"I know you love me, and I know you love your dad. It's fine to love us both, and I'm happy you do."

Your children might wonder:	*You might respond:*
"Does it hurt your feelings that I still love Daddy?"	"I'm glad you love Daddy and want to be with him. Both Daddy and I love you very much, and we always will."
"Should I try not to talk about how much fun I had at Mom's?"	"I know you like to be with Mom, and it's okay to tell me about the good time you had. It makes me happy when you and Mom have fun together."
"Did Mom have an affair?" "Did Dad have a girlfriend before you got divorced?"	"We decided to get divorced for all kinds of grown-up reasons. Some of those reasons are private and just between Dad and Mom."

"You don't have to worry about money"

Reassure children that you will take care of their needs.

After a divorce, the standard of living decreases for most families. Many endure a period of significant financial hardship. In addition, both parents usually have to work outside the home, even if they didn't before the divorce. Financial adjustments and strains affect children as well as adults. Although their understanding of finances is rudimentary, kids know that money is necessary to live and to buy things. They also know—and worry—when their standard of living changes.

Shield children from financial fears

Because of their overriding need for security and stability during and after a divorce, it's important to shield children from financial worries. Experts who work with divorcing families agree that discussing finances with children isn't a wise idea. It is, of course, appropriate for children to understand that both their parents are financially responsible for them and are helping out. But don't share specific information, such as how much your salary is, what you pay for rent, how much their other parent makes, or what the amount of child support is. These are adult matters, and discussing them is likely to confuse and worry children.

If a parent isn't meeting financial obligations, it's best for children not to know. Don't enlist children in an attempt to get a parent to

76

begin paying or to be more timely. Avoid giving them the impression that you blame the other parent for the money situation, even if the blame is warranted. Messages like, "Ask your father—he's the one with the money" or "Ask your mother—that's why I pay child support," put children in the middle and can cause them to feel worried and guilty. On the other hand, if your ex-partner pays regularly and on time, it doesn't hurt to tell your kids that this parent can be relied on to help financially in both homes. It's a reassuring message.

Guidelines for handling money matters with children

Here are some suggestions for helping your kids accept and adjust to a changed financial situation.

1. **Answer questions as they come up.** In general, wait for questions about financial matters before volunteering any information. Respond calmly to questions about money, telling children that there's not as much money in the family now but that there will be enough to meet their needs.

2. **Be matter-of-fact about what's affordable.** It *is* important to make clear to children what you can and can't afford. If children know what's possible and what's not, they're less likely to keep hoping for a scooter, computer, or pair of designer sport shoes that they're not going to get. You might say, "Right now we can't afford things that aren't necessities. We can't buy you

those shoes you saw yesterday, but we'll still find a good pair of shoes for school." Talk about the difference between needing and wanting something. Be matter-of-fact in these discussions, so kids see the situation as "how it is" rather than "how sad and frustrating it is." Also suggest and look for ways that children can earn and save money to buy things they especially want.

3. **Avoid buying things you can't afford.** The temptation to make your kids and yourself feel better by buying them things can be strong. If you succumb occasionally, don't worry about it, but beware of letting this become a habit. If your former spouse is lavishing money on the children in what you think is an attempt to buy their affection, don't worry too much about that either. Kids frequently see such conduct for exactly what it is.

4. **Try to keep children involved in familiar activities.** Do all you can to let your children continue participating in favorite pursuits. Children need activities outside of school that help them grow and develop—and they need these all the more when their lives are disrupted by divorce. If your child loves to play hockey, take clarinet lessons, or do gymnastics, try to figure out a way for him to continue. If your finances simply won't stretch far enough, check into scholarships or see if a sliding-scale fee can be arranged. If, despite all your efforts, you find it's not possible for you to afford a particular activity, make it a priority to find another meaningful but less expensive one for him to take part in and enjoy.

5. **Turn a lack of money into an adventure.** Brainstorm less costly substitutes for things kids want you to buy. Invent alternatives. Instead of buying new clothes and toys, spend a Saturday scouring garage and tag sales. Instead of going to video arcades, visit museums on free days. Instead of paying for movies, borrow videos from the library. Instead of eating out, plan creative menus with what's on hand. Play familiar games and make up new ones. Read out loud together. Make up skits. Explore the neighborhood as if it were a trail in a nature park. It can be fun to brainstorm ideas for how to have a great weekend on ten dollars. Encourage your children—and yourself—to put your fertile imaginations to use.

A word about child support

Divorce is expensive. The standard of living for the entire family usually goes down for a period of time after the divorce. It's a good thing to soften the impact on your children as best you can. The purpose of child support is to equalize, as much as possible, the standard of living in both homes. If you're paying child support, the money you provide is for your children, not your former spouse. Still, many parents who pay child support voice frustration that they have no control over the money and how the other parent spends it. It's true that you have no say in how the money is spent once it leaves your hands. You may feel better about this if you focus on the fact that you're paying the money for the good of your children. Each month, think of that check as a gift of love to your kids—and let it go.

If you're the recipient of child-support payments, there are some things you can do to ensure that the checks come regularly and on time. One of the simplest is to bear in mind that the money really *is* for your children. Use it wisely. If the checks consistently arrive, cash them promptly, and be appreciative. Even though it's a legal obligation for your former spouse to pay and to pay on time, a thank-you is always appropriate—and welcome.

When an ex-spouse is not paying child support or has a significant history of late payments, there are remedies. The number of parents who evade this responsibility is large. Each state now has public agencies, usually connected with the local courts, where you can go for help, and has methods in place to help with enforcing child-support orders entered in other states. If you are one of the unfortunate many whose ex-spouse doesn't meet financial obligations, we encourage you to do something about it. Child support is for your children. When the other parent doesn't pay, your children are the losers. So check with your attorney, ask the court to refer you to the appropriate state agency, or contact an organization like the Office of Child Support Enforcement or Child Support Network (see page 118) and do what you can to compel payment. Your children need and deserve this.

Words you might use

You might start by saying:

"Now that we're living in two homes, our money has to go further. We won't be doing some of the things you're used to doing—like eating in restaurants and getting lots of new toys and clothes—as often. But we'll still eat, and you'll still have clothes you need and toys to play with."

Your children might wonder:	*You might respond:*
"Why isn't there as much money as before?" "Why can't we buy things like we used to?"	"Before we lived in one place, so we only paid for one place. It costs more money to have two homes. Even though the money has to pay for more, we still have enough for the things we need, like food and heat.
"Why does Mom have to work now?"	"We need extra money now that we live in two homes, and Mom's new job helps pay for that."

Your children might wonder:	*You might respond:*
"Tommy's dad never pays his child support. Does Dad pay you?"	"Dad and I have an agreement about money. It's between us, and I don't want you to worry about it."
"Will we go bankrupt?"	"No, we won't go bankrupt. We have enough money for the things we need." *Or:* "I don't know if that will happen, but I do know we'll have food, clothes, and a safe, warm place to live." *Also ask:* "Why do you wonder about that?" *(This can help you determine where the worry comes from: maybe another child told your child about bankruptcy; maybe your ex made a remark about it.)*

"You don't have to worry about me"

Don't try to make a child your confidant. Take care of yourself.

Getting divorced is tough. Your lifestyle has changed dramatically. You may be holding two jobs to help make ends meet, working outside your home for the first time in many years, or taking classes to acquire new skills. You're probably doing many tasks that your ex-spouse used to do. You may be dating again as well. On top of all this, you're a single parent—and working hard to be a good one. That's a *lot* of changes all at once.

To say the least, this probably isn't the most stable or pleasant time of your life. Your children know this, and they're probably worrying about you as well as themselves. Children's worries are concrete. You're their safety and security, and as they see the world, if you aren't functioning well, their survival needs may not get met. They may wonder if you can handle things the other parent once took care of, such as transporting them to school and activities or cooking meals. They may also worry about how you're feeling and about whether you're lonely when they aren't with you. It's even possible that they'll misinterpret your calls to them when they're with their other parent, thinking that you're missing them and need them to care for you.

Guidelines for keeping your kids from worrying

Knowing that your children are likely to be worried about you, you'll want to take steps to stave off their fears and concerns. Here are some of the ways you can help.

1. **Assure your children that you can take care of yourself.** Even when your heart is aching and you miss them terribly, your children need you to make the effort to offer plenty of reassurance about this. Tell them that you'll be okay and that they don't need to take care of you.

2. **Don't load children with adult responsibilities.** Many children of divorce who are now adults report that they feel as if they lost their childhood after their parents' breakup. They stopped playing. They started taking care of younger siblings, cooking meals, and coming home to empty houses and apartments. Even though it's a troubled time with lots of stress, kids still need to play and just be kids.

   Of course, it's fine to expect children to help out at home and take on some additional chores. Helping in age-appropriate ways—cleaning their rooms, caring for pets, and taking turns with daily tasks like doing dishes or vacuuming—fosters children's healthy development. But burdening kids with the regular responsibility for preparing meals, baby-sitting, doing everyone's laundry, and handling all the housework is too much to expect— even if children seem to want to do these things. If your children offer to take on adult responsibilities, thank them, tell them you can take care of such things, and suggest more reasonable tasks they can do to help out at home.

3. **Resist the temptation to make your children confidants.** Though you may want to, don't confide in them regarding new

relationships, how you feel about what your former spouse is doing, or other adult matters. No matter how mature your children may appear, discussing these grown-up concerns puts too much pressure on them at a time when they need opportunities to think about their own lives, take care of schoolwork, spend time with friends, and play. Children aren't "short adults"; let them be kids.

4. **Take care of yourself.** If you're not eating or sleeping enough, you'll lack the physical and emotional energy you need for your children. If you're not nurturing yourself and getting support from other adults, you'll be more easily discouraged or overwhelmed. Take care of yourself, no matter how tired you are, how demanding your schedule is, or how pressing your children's needs may be. You're *not* being selfish when you do this—you're helping yourself be a better parent. Love yourself. Be kind to yourself. Forgive yourself. By respecting and meeting your own needs, you demonstrate to your kids, in ways that words cannot, how responsible grown-ups act and live.

One way to do this is by reaching out to other adults. When you're feeling lonely, inadequate, guilty, sad, confused, or scared, call a friend or a sibling. Consider counseling if your financial situation permits. Find a support group. Seek guidance from books. (See pages 114–116 for a list of books to help you cope during and after your divorce.)

Many adults find it difficult to focus on their role as a parent during this time of change. The adjustments are huge for you as well as for your children. You may not believe or even want to hear the words "It will get better," but it will. In the process, it's important to take care of yourself. Try sitting down and writing out a list of things that make you feel good. Think back to your own childhood and what made you feel happy and energetic. Keep your list handy and, every so often, read it and look for ideas to claim a little happiness for yourself right now.

Words you might use

You might start by saying:

"It's nice that you care about how I'm feeling. But you don't have to worry about me—I know how to take care of myself."

"I'm not feeling very good right now. The divorce is really hard for me, too. But even though I feel bad some of the time, I'm taking care of myself. I talk to Dave and to Uncle Matt when I want help figuring something out, and I'm seeing a counselor. I'll get better soon. And no matter how I'm feeling, I will always take care of you."

You might ask:

"Are you worried about how I'm doing?"

"It's nice of you to help out at home, but you're doing too much. What's something fun you could do tonight instead?"

Your children might wonder: *You might respond:*

"Why do you cry so much? Are you going to be okay?"

"I'm sad, and crying helps me feel better. It can feel good to let sad feelings out with tears. I'm really okay, and I don't want you to worry about me."

"Why are the grown-ups so upset? They told us things would be okay, but it doesn't seem like they are."

"The divorce is hard for everyone. I'm sorry if we seem upset—sometimes letting feelings show helps them get better faster. It will take some time, but Dad and I are both okay."

"We won't put you in the middle"

Don't speak ill of the other parent or ask your child to keep secrets. Do your own communicating.

Children of divorce feel deep loyalty conflicts. They want to please both of their parents, and can be torn by guilt if they perceive that they have to choose one parent over the other. Sometimes children unknowingly put themselves in the middle by saying what they think you want to hear. For example, they may complain about their other parent because they believe you get some pleasure from hearing it.

Psychologists tell us that children, at their deepest cores, view themselves as one-half of each parent. This is tremendously important for divorcing parents to understand. To some extent, in criticizing the other parent, children may actually be criticizing *themselves* as well. And when parents criticize one another, imagine what children perceive. For example, suppose your ex-spouse is late to pick up the children and you say, "Your mom is so irresponsible!" What your child may hear is, *"You* are so irresponsible!" It doesn't matter that this isn't what you said—if you express anger at the other parent in front of your children, they may see it as anger toward them. Taken to the extreme, this can mean that if you say, "I hate your father," your child may hear, "I hate *you."*

Set a positive stance toward your ex

Do all that you can to make positive statements about your ex-spouse. A good rule of thumb to follow is this: *It never hurts to say something good about the other parent, and it always hurts to say something bad.*

When your children say good things about their other parent, agree with those statements if you can find it in you. Also make it clear that you don't want to hear criticisms of the other parent from your kids. Of course, it's impossible to predict specifically what derogatory things your children might say about the other parent. Usually such statements take the form of complaints about living with that parent. Your children may complain about being bored ("There's nothing to do over there"). They may not like the rules at the other home ("Dad doesn't let me listen to my music as loud as I want"). They may not have the same material goods ("There's no computer to play games on"). In cases like these, there's not much you can do to control what happens in your ex-partner's home. (See "If a child needs protection," page 68, for suggestions on what to do if a child tells you about dangerous conditions or if you suspect there are serious problems.) What you *can* do for your children is demonstrate that adults draw boundaries and enforce them. When a child complains to you about the other parent, encourage her to talk with that parent about what's bothering her. You might say, "Sounds like you're mad at Dad. That's something you need to talk about with him."

This is a message that you may have to repeat many times in many contexts. It can help to keep in mind that when the roles are reversed, as they inevitably will be, you'll want your ex-spouse to foster respect and love for you.

Here are other tips for avoiding and redirecting negative comments about the other parent:

DON'T

- quiz your child about what's going on at the other parent's home. If you need or want to know something, ask your former spouse directly.

- ask children to take sides in any argument you have with the other parent.

- ask your kids who they'd rather live with or who they like best.

DO

- explore what's really happening when a child complains about the other parent. To find out, check with your ex about what's going on. You might say, "Kira keeps complaining about the sleeping arrangements at your place. I told her she should talk to you about it, but I wanted to make sure you knew. Do you think there's a problem?" If verbal communication is difficult for you, do this reality check in writing.

Don't ask your children to keep secrets

It is common for divorced parents to ask their children to keep secrets from the other parent: "Don't tell Daddy we're going on a trip." "Don't tell Mom about my girlfriend." "Don't tell your father I bought that." Divorced parents are entitled to a certain amount of privacy about their personal lives, but asking your child to keep secrets isn't the way to acquire and maintain this privacy.

Why? For one thing, asking a child to keep a secret is frequently a surefire way to make certain the secret *is* revealed. The result is that the child feels worse than ever—guilty about being asked to hide something from the other parent *and* about having disclosed the secret.

Second, by asking your child to keep a secret, you are teaching him to lie or mislead. The underlying lesson is that deceit is acceptable. Your child may internalize that lesson and think it's okay to lie to you or others.

It's natural and healthy for you to want much of your life to be unknown to your ex-spouse. Unfortunately, though, it's difficult for divorced parents to carve out a zone of privacy for themselves. In your kids' experience, when the two of you were living together, you welcomed hearing about what each child did with the other parent when you were absent. Now that you're apart, your children won't necessarily stop sharing information. It can be helpful to tell your kids that you don't expect them to tell you everything that's going on in the other home. To protect your own privacy, though, your safest strategy is to avoid saying or doing anything when your kids are present that you don't want your ex to know about. It's wise to assume that anything you do or say in their presence will be reported in one form or another (and not always accurately) to their other parent. This can also mean that you'll need to accept having your ex-partner know more about your life than you'd prefer. Difficult as this may be, take heart in knowing that your child isn't feeling burdened with secrets.

Do your own communicating

It can be tempting to have your children deliver messages to the other parent, especially if communicating with your ex is difficult for you.

Asking your child to "have your father call me" or "give your mom this check" may seem like a harmless thing to do, but consider these kinds of requests from your children's perspective: What if they forget to deliver a message? What happens if they lose an envelope? What if the other parent won't like hearing the message? Will they have to bring a message back? It's best for both children and grown-ups when parents communicate directly without involving their kids. When you do this, you're modeling respect, responsibility, and self-accountability. Most important, you're keeping your kids out of the middle of parental communications.

Parents often comment that if they could work together and communicate, they would still be married. The reality is that good communication takes hard work, but it's worth the effort. If you're tempted to have one of your children deliver a message to the other parent, stop and ask yourself why you don't want to convey the message yourself.

It bears repeating that if you and your spouse are having disagreements during or after your divorce, consider using mediation as a means to resolve your issues. Mediation can save much time and money. It's also less stressful than the adversarial process used in courts. Mediators aren't judges; they don't make decisions for you. Their role is to help the two of you reach agreements. There are many advantages to mediation, the primary one being that you and your ex-partner are in charge of your agreements. Surrendering power and decision-making authority to a stranger in a black robe should always be the last resort. You know your children better than anyone else. In addition, studies have shown that people are more likely to abide by agreements for which they've been part of the decision-making process rather than ones that were forced on them by a judge. Even if you're unable to agree about property divisions and child-support amounts, you'll do your family a great service if you can mediate a time-sharing arrangement for your children. Sometimes these arrangements need to be renegotiated as children grow or as your adult situations change, and mediation can help at these stages as well.

Divorce Rules for Parents Written by Their Children*

1. No bribing or spoiling to hurt the other parent.
2. No name calling.
3. No fighting.
4. No hurting each other.
5. No fighting over the kids.
6. No calling on the phone and yelling.
7. No carrying messages through the kids. Do your own communicating with notes, letters, or calls.
8. Share money equally.
9. Keep personal business like money and problems to yourself.
10. Don't blame kids for your problems.
11. No bad-mouthing the other parent to anybody.
12. No throwing or breaking things.
13. Don't get mad at the kids for your money problems.

---

* Drafted and approved by the Longfellow Elementary School Divorce Adjustment Group, Albuquerque, New Mexico. The children, ages seven to eleven, wrote these rules after sitting through some courtroom divorce proceedings.

A reasonable goal for divorced parents is to achieve a businesslike relationship with one another. This doesn't mean you have to like or approve of each other. But it does mean polite dialogue. It means timely payments of child support. It means sharing important information on a prompt basis. It means attending important school functions. It means cooperative parenting.

If your ex puts your kids in the middle

Sometimes, despite one parent's best efforts, the other parent refuses to cooperate. What can you do if your ex-spouse continues to put your children in the middle?

- Focus on your children and their needs. If a child asks, "Why does Mommy say you're a bad father?" you might reply, "Mommy's angry with me. I don't think she realizes how hard it is for you to hear her say those things about me." Then talk about what the child can do or say to handle the situation in the future. Your child might tell the other parent, "I feel upset when you say bad things about Daddy. Please don't do that anymore."

- Keep confidentiality. Telling the other parent what your children have said can put kids back in the middle.

- If you need to vent or discuss your concerns with someone, talk to a trusted friend or another adult. This will let you safely release your anger without further involving your kids.

Words you might use

You might start by saying:

> "I hear you saying that you don't like the food at Mom's house. I can understand your feelings about that. But Mom is responsible for you when you're with her, just like I'm responsible when you're with me. So the best thing for you to do is talk to her about it. It's something that is just between Mom and you."

> "Your mother and I are divorced now. That means that we won't be sharing as much as we did before. You don't need to tell me what's going on in her life unless it's really important to you. She's taking care of herself, and I'm taking care of me, so it's okay for you not to tell me stuff about her."

> "It's all right with me if you want to talk with Dad about what's happening when you're here with me. But remember that if there's something going on here that you don't like, he can't do as much about it as I can. If you're having any problems when you're here, please tell me, because I'm in charge here and I'm the one who can help in this home."

You might ask:

"Are you feeling torn or stuck in the middle? Can you tell me why?"

"What do you think you can do if you don't like something here or at your father's place?"

Your children might wonder:

"You told me I could talk about my feelings, so why won't you listen to me complain about Mommy?" "What can I do if I wish something was different at Mommy's home?"

You might respond:

"Some things are best to talk about with me, and some things with Mommy. You need to talk to Mommy if you have a problem with her. She's the one who can help when you're bothered about something that happens when you're at home with her."

Your children might wonder:	*You might respond:*
"Do I have to pick sides?"	"No. We don't want you to pick sides. We both love you, and we won't put you in the middle our grown-up problems."
"Can't you and Daddy talk to each other? I don't want to be a messenger."	"You're right—it's no fun to be a messenger, and you don't have to be one. I won't ask you to tell Daddy stuff for me anymore. And I'll talk to Daddy about that, too."

"We are still a family"

Help children understand that their changing family is still a family. Keep the connections to extended family.

With divorce, children may feel that they've lost their family. It's important to reassure them that they do indeed still have a family. Explain that the chief difference after the divorce is that the family now has two homes. Even if your children aren't seeing the other parent, hearing you say that they still have a family is comforting to most children.

The idea of family gets more complicated when parents remarry. Frequently children find themselves with new stepbrothers and stepsisters as well as new stepparents. Younger children in particular are likely to be confused. Help children see that they remain in one family but now also have an additional one. (For more on stepfamilies, see "Our life is changing," pages 103–107.) Talk with children about the many different kinds of families in the world: small and large, two-parent and single-parent, extended families, stepfamilies. Explain that a family is a group of people who live together and care for and about each other.

During and after your divorce, make an extra effort to foster children's relationships with other members of your family and your former ex-spouse's family. Continuing contact with grandparents, uncles, aunts, and cousins is critical right now. These connections reinforce for children the fact that the divorce did not end their family. The security of knowing what family or group they belong to can go a long way toward helping your kids cope with the divorce now as well as with their own adult relationships when they are grown.

Grandparents are especially important

A big question on many children's minds is, "What about my grand-parents?" As the storm of divorce churns through their lives, children need the anchor of their grandparents' support. They need to know how, if at all, their relationship with their grandparents will change as a result of the divorce. Moreover, they'll be watching the adults to see how they're feeling about one another.

Your parents may be ready to scream at your ex-spouse. You are their child, and they may feel, rightly or wrongly, that you've been betrayed. They may blame the entire divorce on your ex. They may be so angry that they'll refuse to speak to him or her, and at the same time feel betrayed themselves, especially if they truly loved your spouse. The other set of parents may feel exactly the same way about you. Sometimes, too, parents of divorcing couples become angry or disappointed with their adult children for making the decision to end the marriage. At the very least, both sets of grandparents are likely to feel sad about what has happened.

In this emotional maelstrom, your children are at risk. They love their grandparents. They love their parents. They need the security that such love provides. You *and* your parents have an obligation to protect your children from the adult issues that accompany a divorce.

It will help your children if both you and your spouse talk with your respective parents. Tell them how important they are to your children. Remind them how important both of *you* are to your children, too. Share with them the information contained in this book. Make sure they understand that what you want most of all is for them to love your children and to not say *anything* derogatory to the children about your former spouse. Tell them to refer any questions about the divorce to you.

The second thing you can do to help your children is talk to your former in-laws yourself. Tell them you know how important they are to your children. Promise you won't undermine their relationship with their grandkids. You can also ask them not to say or do anything that could convey to the children that they're displeased with you. Many grandparents are happy to help and will appreciate the guidance you give them.

You might say: "Both of us are committed to doing as much as we can to help the kids get through the divorce. We'd both really appreciate your help. You can help the kids by just being there for them, by listening and supporting and loving them.

"We also ask that you not say anything bad about either one of us to the kids. They need to know that we both love them and will take care of them. It's a really stressful time for them, and we don't want them to feel that one of us is at fault for the divorce or that one of us isn't a good person. We know you're sad and angry, but please talk to *us* about that, not to the kids. We're both going to cooperate in raising the kids, and we really appreciate your help and understanding."

Use the same language to talk with other adults in your children's lives. Your friends and family want to know how they can help. All of these people can provide wonderful support for your kids, especially if they know that you want them in your children's lives.

There are times when other adults, especially grandparents, aren't willing to cooperate the way you need them to. In this situation, you may need to take additional steps such as remaining with the children during their visits. Don't hesitate to consult a counselor or mediator to help you figure out what to do. In extreme cases, you might have to seek help from the court that issued the divorce.

Words you might use

You might start by saying:

"Parents divorce each other—they don't divorce children. We are still a family, and we always will be. We're still your parents, and we always will be. Your sisters and brothers will always be your sisters and brothers, too. Nothing can change any of that.

"Your grandparents are still your family, too. Even though we're divorced, Grandma and Grandpa and Grammy and Granddad still love you as much as they ever did! Their special feelings for you haven't changed at all."

You might ask:

"Who are the people in your family?"
(Have children draw a family tree.)

"Do you understand that you still have a family?"

Your children might wonder:	*You might respond:*
"Will I still see Nana and Gramps?"	"Yes. Nana and Gramps will still visit you, talk to you, and take you places. You can still stay overnight at their apartment."
"Why is Grandma mad at Dad?"	"Grandma's upset about the divorce. She thought Dad and I would always be together. She somehow feels the divorce is Dad's fault, but it isn't. Dad and I decided together to get a divorce. It's hard for Grandma to understand that, though. And I know Grandma still wants you to love your dad."

"Our life is changing"

When you or your ex-spouse form a new partnership, your children will be watching every move you make and listening to every word you say.

It's wise not to rush the process of bringing a new significant adult into children's lives. Do this gradually, allowing everyone time to get to know one another. The more careful groundwork you lay, the more likely it is that your children will accept the relationship—an incalculable benefit to everyone involved.

Early romances—those intense ones that happen soon after a separation—are often destined not to last. If you're dating but your relationship isn't a commitment, it's wise not to introduce your children to a new casual friend or to encourage them to get close to the person. Wait till you know the connection is probably going to be permanent. This protects your children from experiencing yet another loss in their lives.

New partnerships affect children

If your former spouse is in a new relationship, your children need your permission for them to like and eventually love this new adult in their lives. Painful as it may be, giving this permission is key to your children's happiness and security. As long as they know they have your genuine permission to like this new adult, they'll decide for themselves how they feel. Don't interfere. Remember that you'll want and need the same courtesy from your ex-spouse when you bring a new partner into your family.

If you have found a new partner, it's important that your ex get this news from you, not from the children. Tell your former spouse first: it's respectful to do so, and a private notification gives both of you the opportunity to prepare yourselves and to plan how to talk with your children about it. Even a written note is better than not relaying this information at all.

A second marriage presents tremendous challenges for you, your ex, your children, your new partner, and the new adult's children. As important as it is to you that your next marriage succeed, it may be more important for your children. Going through another breakup could be harder for them than the first. This next relationship has a much greater chance of survival if you have at least the tacit support of your children's other parent.

Give your children information and reassurance about the new situation. They'll wonder whether their rooms will be the same, how their routines will change, and if you'll still love them as much as before. It's not uncommon for children to fear that since you have a new person in your life, you may have stopped loving them. Tell them you still love them as much as ever. Be sure to spend one-on-one time with each of your kids. Give them lots of reassurance about what will be happening. Let them know how important they are to you and that this will never change.

Explain a new adult's role in children's lives

Think carefully about exactly what the new adult's role will be in your children's lives. Explain this role clearly to your children. They need to know that a stepparent will never replace their actual mother or father. If you're the first one to bring a stepparent or significant other into the family, it's up to you to help children understand that this person will have a unique place and won't change or push aside their connection to their actual parents. For instance, if you're forming a commitment to another man, talk with him about how you expect him to relate to your kids. Explain to the children that he won't take their father's place. He's another adult who will care for them and give them guidance, but their father is still their father.

In some cases, the new adult *will* take on the role of father or mother. If, for example, one parent abandoned the children, or if a new stepparent adopts them, they may perceive the stepparent as an actual parent. However, if your children's other parent is involved in their lives, it's usually wise for the stepparent to carve out a different relationship.

Explain to the children that you love this person and that she or he is bringing you joy and fulfillment as an adult. Assure them that your new partner will never replace them and that you will always love and care for them. Expect that they will have insecurities about this, even if they don't say so directly.

Words you might use

You might start by saying:

"I want to tell you something important. My relationship with Barry is getting serious. It feels like we might want to get married someday, but we all need a chance to get used to that idea. You and I need lots of time to talk about it so I can answer all your questions. I want you to know that I will always love you and care for you—nothing about my new relationship can ever change that."

"I hear from Dad that you're going to have a new stepmom. I think that's great. Stepmoms can be really neat people and I bet Saundra will be. I know she'll care for you a lot, because you're very special. You know, I'll always be your mom and I'll always love you, but it's okay with me if Saundra loves you, too. I want your dad to be happy, and I want you to be happy. I'll be glad if you like or love your new stepmom, so please don't wonder about that."

You might ask:

"Are you wondering what's going on with me?"

"What do you think it will be like to have a stepbrother?"

Your children might wonder:	***You might respond:***
"Mom, is Michael your boyfriend? Do you think you'll get married?"	"I'm dating Michael. He's a nice person and we have fun together. Right now I'm just getting to know him, and I'm not ready to get married again yet. I don't know what will happen, but please don't worry. I'll tell you if it gets serious and we'll talk about it. You can ask me about it anytime you want."
"Dad, when you get married, will I have two moms?"	"You'll still have one mom. Renee won't ever be your mother— she'll be your stepmother, and that's different. Renee will be another adult who loves you, but she won't replace Mom."
"What if I don't like living in a stepfamily?"	"A change like this can be scary and upsetting, and I suppose it's possible that you *won't* like living in your new stepfamily at first. I think you will, though— and I know you'll get used to it and like it someday. A stepfamily means more people to love you and more for you to love, too."

Some final words

The divorce is an episode in your life. It is not your life. The same is true for your children. There is great wisdom and peace in the words "This too shall pass." Remind yourself and your children that the current turmoil will pass, and pass it will. You and your children will get through the divorce. A year from now, things will be better.

You can greet the world each day with fear or with trust. Whichever you choose, your children will observe and learn from you. If you demonstrate that you face life with hope and confidence, they will strive to do this also. Knowing they are loved and in good hands enables them to meet the world with optimism, not anxiety. That is a great gift of love.

Change is inevitable in life. Wherever the winds of life blow your children, they will be equipped to weather the storms. And they will remember. They will remember that in a moment of great challenge, sadness, and turmoil, you taught them to greet each day with trust, love, and confidence—not fear.

A divorce glossary

Here is an alphabetical list of words and basic definitions for children that you may find useful. Terminology varies from state to state, and your state may use different language in some cases.

alimony: Money that one parent pays the other parent to help with home or school expenses. When people are married, sometimes one parent has a job that pays for most or all of the things the family needs. After a divorce, if the other parent doesn't have enough money to live on or needs extra money, that parent might get alimony. Alimony isn't paid in every divorce. When it is, often the dad pays alimony to the mom.

child support: Money that one parent gives the other parent to help pay for things their kids need while they are growing up.

counselor: A woman or man who talks to people about their feelings and helps them solve their problems and feel better. With divorce, children and parents sometimes want help understanding and dealing with their feelings or figuring out what to do. A counselor can help them do this. The counselor might talk to one of the parents or one child alone, or to parents or whole families together. A counselor might also be called a therapist, psychotherapist, clinical social worker, psychologist, or mental therapist.

court: A place where parents go to get their divorce or to have a judge help them if they need it. Sometimes children might go to court, too, if that can help the judge decide how to help their parents.

custody: A word that defines how parents make decisions for their children. In many divorces, both parents make important decisions together about their children. This arrangement may also be called *joint custody* or *shared custody.* When one parent is in charge of making the decisions, some states call that *sole custody.*

divorce: A legal word for the end of a marriage. Parents who get divorced aren't married to each other any longer. They sign legal papers saying that the marriage is over and they won't be living in the same home.

divorce decree: The paper that has all the legal agreements the grown-ups made about the divorce. It is sometimes called a *settlement agreement.*

judge: A man or woman who makes decisions for people who can't agree on their own. A judge can help parents decide what's best for children, such as who will have custody and when kids will live in which home. A judge might also help parents make other decisions about the divorce, like how to divide their property and money.

lawyer: A woman or man who helps one parent or the other with the legal details of the divorce. Usually the mom has her own lawyer and the dad has his own lawyer. A lawyer goes with the mom or dad to court to talk to the judge.

mediator: A man or a woman who sits down with both parents and helps them work out the details of their divorce.

separation: An arrangement where parents decide to live apart but not get divorced. Sometimes people who do this will have an agreement written up, and this can be called a *legal separation.*

settlement agreement: The paper that has all the legal agreements the grown-ups made about the divorce. It is sometimes called a *divorce decree.*

supervised visitation: A legal arrangement where a parent may see his or her children with another adult (such as a family member, counselor, social worker, or friend) nearby.

time-sharing: A term that describes how parents will spend time with their children. Sometimes one parent might have the children more of the time and can have what is called *physical custody* while the other parent has *visitation.*

Resources for you and your family

Books to share with your children

Dear Mr. Henshaw by Beverly Cleary (New York: Harper-Collins, 1994). This story is written as a series of letters and diary entries addressed to a young boy's favorite author. In his letters, ten-year-old Leigh reveals his problems in coping with his parents' divorce, being the new boy in school, and generally finding his own place in the world. Ages 9–12.

Goodbye, Hello: Everything You Need to Help Your Child When Your Family Moves by Anna McDonnell (Santa Monica, CA: Two Rivers Inc., 1997). This is a clever moving kit to help children. It includes a booklet, change-of-address cards, a calendar, pictures drawn by other children who have moved, moving reminders, and a journal. Ages 3–12.

How It Feels When Parents Divorce by Jill Krementz (New York: Alfred A Knopf, 1988). Nineteen boys and girls, ages seven to sixteen and from diverse backgrounds, share their deepest feelings about their parents' divorce. In reading their stories, you and your family will discover that all children of divorced parents can find positive ways to help themselves through this difficult time. You'll learn that your feelings of anger, confusion, and pain have been experienced by others and are normal. Ages 7–18.

I Don't Want to Talk About It by Jeanie Franz Ransom (Washington, DC: Magination Press, 2000). In this wonderfully illustrated story, a girl's parents tell her they're getting divorced. The book presents an excellent example of how to tell children about divorce. Ages 4–8.

I Hate Goodbyes! by Kathleen C. Szaj (Mahwah, NJ: Paulist Press 1997). A little girl who hates good-byes and tries to ignore her feelings learns how to make the separations in her life easier. Ages 4–8.

It's Not the End of the World by Judy Blume (New York: Yearling Books, 1986). Karen has decided she'll never get married. All her parents do is fight, and now they're talking about divorce. At first Karen is sure they can work it out if they try, but after meeting a friend whose parents are also divorced, Karen starts to rethink whether her parents staying together is really the best solution. Ages 9–12.

My Family's Changing: A First Look at Family Break Up by Pat Thomas (Hauppauge NY: Barrons Educational Series Inc., 1999). The author of this picture book for young children, a psychotherapist, guides children through their fears, questions, and worries during a divorce. Ages 4–8.

My Parents Still Love Me Even Though They're Getting Divorced: An Interactive Tale for Children by Lois V. Nightingale (Yorba Linda, CA: Nightingale Rose, 1997). This book for parents and children to use together includes pictures to color and multiple-choice questions to help children feel reassured, nurtured, and loved. Ages 4–8.

When Your Parents Split Up: How to Keep Yourself Together by Alys Swan-Jackson (New York: Price Stern Sloan, 1998). This guide for teens offers expert advice for surviving divorce, handling change, dealing with parents, and coping with feelings. Includes questionnaires, activities, resources, and interviews with real teens. Ages 12–18.

Books for adults

Between Love and Hate: A Guide to Civilized Divorce by Lois Gold (New York: Plume, 1996). The book provides tools for couples to handle the divorce process peacefully, suggests ways of working cooperatively as parents, offers conflict-resolution strategies, and discusses the emotional needs of children during their parents' divorce.

Beyond Blame: A New Way of Resolving Conflicts in Relationships by Jeffrey Kottler (San Francisco: Jossey-Bass, 1996). An excellent resource for learning how to resolve conflicts without blaming others, this book teaches ways to react more positively and effectively to difficult situations.

The Budget Kit: The Common Cents Money Management Workbook by Judy Lawrence (Chicago: Dearborn Trade, 2000). This simple and easy-to-use money management book can help you get your financial house in order.

Child Behavior: The Classic Childcare Manual from the Gesell Institute of Human Development by Frances L. Ilg, Louise Bates Ames, and Stanley M. Baker (New York: HarperPerennial, 1992). This authoritative and respected guide offers the basics of child development and covers a wide variety of issues including divorce.

Child Custody: Building Parenting Agreements that Work by Mimi E. Lyster (Berkeley, CA: Nolo.com, 2000). An excellent source for developing parenting agreements, this book includes sample agreements that can help you decide things you want in yours.

Crazy Time: Surviving Divorce and Building a New Life by Abigail Trafford (New York: HarperPerennial, 1992). A straightforward guide for surviving the emotional storms of divorce, this book contains many real-life stories and examples of adults coping with the crazy time. After *Mom's House, Dad's House* (see page 116), this is the next book you should read.

The Divorce Recovery Sourcebook by Dawn Bradley Berry (Lincolnwood, IL: NTC Publishing Group, 1999). Here's a source of general divorce information such as finding a good lawyer, receiving a fair settlement, and working out a custody arrangement.

Does Wednesday Mean Mom's House or Dad's? Parenting Together While Living Apart by Marc J. Ackerman (New York: John Wiley & Sons, 1996). This book gives parents clear, practical guidelines for coparenting and handling transitions between two homes.

Helping Children Cope with Divorce by Edward Teyber (San Francisco: Jossey-Bass, 2001). This is a useful reference on what children may be thinking, feeling, and needing during the stages of divorce, and how parents can help.

Helping Your Grandchildren Through Their Parents' Divorce by Joan Schrager Cohen (New York: Walker & Co., 1994). This book explains to grandparents the needs of their grandchildren during divorce.

Helping Your Kids Cope with Divorce the Sandcastles Way by M. Gary Neuman with Patricia Romanowski (New York: Random House, 1999). One of the best and most comprehensive books for divorcing parents, this is a good reference to have by your side. It contains many activities to help children express feelings, and offers guidelines on living arrangements and time-sharing based on children's ages and developmental needs. The book presents too much information to absorb at a single reading; when questions or issues arise, go to the index, then read about your specific concerns.

How to Talk So Kids Will Listen & Listen So Kids Will Talk by Adele Faber and Elaine Mazlish. (New York: Avon Books, 1999). Here's a wonderful step-by-step guide to help parents talk and problem-solve with their children ages 4 and up.

Joint Custody with a Jerk: Raising a Child with an Uncooperative Ex by Julie A. Ross and Judy Corcoran (New York: St. Martin's Press, 1996). This terrific guide for learning communication techniques to help deal with a difficult ex also teaches how to look at your own role in the problem.

Mom's House, Dad's House: Making Two Homes for Your Child: A Complete Guide for Parents Who Are Separated, Divorced, or Remarried by Isolina Ricci (New York: Fireside, 1997). If you read only one book besides *Speaking of Divorce,* this should be it. It's one of the best books on developing a successful two-home parenting arrangement. The author discusses the legal, financial, and emotional realities of creating two happy, stable homes for children.

101 Ways to Be a Long-Distance Super Dad or Mom, Too! by George Newman (Tucson, AZ: Blossom Valley Press, 1997). This is a book full of great suggestions for ways to stay in touch when one parent lives far away.

Vicki Lansky's Divorce Book for Parents: Helping Your Children Cope with Divorce and Its Aftermath by Vicki Lansky (Minnetonka, MN: Book Peddlers, 1996). This is a practical, easy-to-understand guide for parenting after divorce, with helpful information about talking to children and about the realities of custody and child support. It also contains many helpful resources.

"Why Did You Have to Get a Divorce? And When Can I Get a Hamster?" ***A Guide for Parenting Through Divorce*** by Anthony E. Wolf (New York: Noonday Press, 1998). Wolf offers practical guidelines and advice on talking about divorce. The book sets out strategies for keeping kids out of the middle of adult disputes. It may also help you if you have an uncooperative ex-spouse.

Wonderful Ways to Be a Stepparent by Judy Ford and Anna Chase (Berkeley, CA: Conari Press, 1999). This book contains practical, concrete advice for developing a harmonious stepfamily.

Organizations and Web sites

Association for Conflict Resolution
1527 New Hampshire Avenue NW
Washington, DC 20036
(202) 667-9700
www.mediators.org

The largest organization of family mediators and a good source for locating one, this is a merged organization of Academy of Family Mediators, Conflict Resolution Education Network, and Society of Professionals in Dispute Resolution. Provides lots of information about the mediation process.

American Academy of Matrimonial Lawyers
150 North Michigan Avenue, Suite 2040
Chicago, IL 60601
(312) 263-6477
www.aaml.org

An organization composed of attorneys specializing in family law. Provides a list of members as well as various publications. A good source for finding a knowledgeable attorney.

American Association of Marriage and Family Therapy
1133 15th Street NW, Suite 300
Washington, DC 20005-2710
(202) 452-0109
www.aamft.org

AAMFT provides referrals to marriage and family therapists in local areas and publishes a consumer's guide to marriage and family therapy.

National Domestic Violence Hotline
P.O. Box 161810
Austin, TX 78716
1-800-799-SAFE (1-800-799-7233)
www.ndvh.org
Provides callers with crisis intervention, information about domestic violence, and referrals to local programs twenty-four hours a day, seven days a week.

Office of Child Support Enforcement
370 L'Enfant Promenade SW
Washington, DC 20447
(202) 401-9370
www.acf.dhhs.gov/programs/cse/
A federal/state/local partnership program that can be a resource for ensuring enforcement of child support orders.

Stepfamily Association of America
650 J Street, Suite 205
Lincoln, NE 68508
1-800-735-0329
www.saafamilies.org
A national nonprofit membership organization dedicated to successful stepfamily living.

www.childsupport.com
Web site of Child Support Network, a specialized service company designed to locate missing parents and collect and enforce court-ordered child-support payments.

www.divorcenet.com
A good resource site about divorce. Has a state-by-state guide as well as lots of bulletin boards and helpful articles.

www.experts.com
An excellent site with an exhaustive list of resources for all kinds of parenting issues, not just divorce.

www.makinglemonade.com
Offers both male and female single parents a place to find support, information, creativity, and a good chuckle. The site offers links to single parenting resources, bulletin boards, poetry, stories, email chat groups, and a bimonthly newsletter.

www.rosemond.com
This site for John Rosemond, a noted parenting expert, features weekly columns, a question and answer of the week, parenting stories, resource directories, weekly polls, and more.

www.sandcastlesprogram.com
A good site with lots of information about parenting after divorce. Has a discussion forum for kids.

Index

About the authors

Roberta Beyer is a lawyer and mediator who helps families through the divorce process. She has always wanted to help kids whose parents are getting divorced, and in 1995, she created a calendar with stickers so kids and parents could keep track of their schedules. Since then, she has developed other products, and along with Kent Winchester, she also wrote *What in the World Do You Do When Your Parents Divorce? A Survival Guide for Kids*. She's the creator of The "Keep Track" Calendar for Kids and The Mom & Dad Pad. Roberta's favorite things to do are fly-fishing, gardening, and cooking. She lives in Albuquerque, New Mexico, with her two border collies, Fly and Jenny, whom she loves to spoil.

Kent Winchester is a trial lawyer who helps women who are sexually harassed and people who are treated unfairly by big corporations. He's the father of two children, Ian and Shauna. He loves to backpack, fly-fish, and read. Kent is the coauthor of *What in the World Do You Do When Your Parents Divorce? A Survival Guide for Kids,* with Roberta Beyer, and is the author of the *Magic Words Handbook for Kids*. He lives in New Mexico and also has two border collies.

Other Materials from Free Spirit Publishing

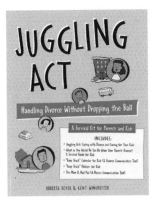

JUGGLING ACT KIT
Handling Divorce
Without Dropping the Ball:
A Survival Kit for Parents and Kids
This comprehensive kit includes the parents' book, kids' book, Mom & Dad Pad with mailing envelopes, calendar, and stickers. For parents and caregivers of children 12 and under. *$49.95; box is 10" x 13"*

WHAT IN THE WORLD DO YOU DO WHEN YOUR PARENTS DIVORCE?
A Survival Guide for Kids
by Kent Winchester and Roberta Beyer
This book uses simple words and affirmations to help children work through fear, confusion, sadness, anger, and other painful emotions caused by divorce.
$9.95; 128 pp.; softcover; illus.; 6" x 6"

THE MOM & DAD PAD
A Divorce Communication Tool

Divorced parents can use the forms to notify each other about school events, appointments, transportation arrangements, travel plans, and other scheduling issues. For parents and caregivers. *$15.95; 25 forms with carbonless copies; 25 mailing envelopes; 8¹/2" x 11"*

"KEEP TRACK" CALENDAR FOR KIDS

Kids can fill in this blank calendar with notes and stickers to remind them which parent they'll be with on which days, and helps them keep track of special events, holidays, appointments, homework, and activities. For ages 7–12. *$9.95; 8¹/2" x 11"*

"KEEP TRACK" STICKERS FOR KIDS

Kids can use these colorful stickers to mark holidays, school activities, and other special dates in calendars. For ages 7–12. *$9.95; set of 400 stickers; each sticker is approximately 1" x 1"*

To place an order or to request a free catalog of SELF–HELP FOR KIDS® *and* SELF–HELP FOR TEENS® *materials, please write, call, email, or visit our Web site:*

Free Spirit Publishing Inc.
217 Fifth Avenue North • Suite 200 • Minneapolis, MN 55401-1299
toll-free 800.735.7323 • local 612.338.2068 • fax 612.337.5050
help4kids@freespirit.com • www.freespirit.com

Visit us on the Web!
www.freespirit.com

Stop by anytime to find our Parents' Choice Approved catalog with fast, easy, secure 24-hour online ordering; "Ask Our Authors," where visitors ask questions—and authors give answers—on topics important to children, teens, parents, teachers, and others who care about kids; links to other Web sites we know and recommend; fun stuff for everyone, including quick tips and strategies from our books; and much more! Plus our site is completely searchable so you can find what you need in a hurry. Stop in and let us know what you think!

Just point and click!

 Get the first look at our books, catch the latest news from Free Spirit, and check out our site's newest features.

contact Do you have a question for us or for one of our authors? Send us an email. Whenever possible, you'll receive a response within 48 hours.

order! Order in confidence! Our secure server uses the most sophisticated online ordering technology available. And ordering online is just one of the ways to purchase our books: you can also order by phone, fax, or regular mail. No matter which method you choose, excellent service is our goal.

1.800.735.7323 • fax 612.337.5050 • help4kids@freespirit.com